ACCELERATED SUCCESS

STAN WILLIAMS

PUBLISHED BY WAVECREST

Published by Wavecrest
307 Orchard City Drive
Suite 210
Campbell California 95008 United States
info@fastpencil.com
(408) 540-7571
(408) 540-7572 (Fax)
http://wavecrest.fastpencil.com

Printed in the United States of America.

First Edition

It is with great joy that I have the opportunity to acknowledge those who have stood with me on this journey.

~

My wife, Dee: Thank you for always supporting me and allowing me to be the Man of God that He has called me to be.

~

My children, Stanley Jr. and Camielle (Chavis): You have been great, awesome examples for the next generation thanks for supporting your dad.

~

My mother, Elder Betty Moon: You have always been an inspiration and great support in my life and ministry.

~

Sister Anita Bonaparte: Thank you for being steadfast in making sure that everything needed, to make this book come to life, was provided.

૭ઈ

Acknowledgments

To Minister Wanda Moore, my spiritual daughter: You have been a greater blessing than you will ever know. Your character speaks volumes to whom and whose you are.

CONTENTS

FOREWORD

In difficult times, it is essential to receive a confirming Word from God through men of God and men of faith. When Israel faced enemies who sought to destroy them, they lost all hope. But, God spoke through the prophet Jahaziel to reassure Israel that "the battle is not yours, but God's." (2 Chronicles 20:15 KJV)

It was this Word that gave Israel renewed strength and a strategy for victory. In a moment, they went from fearful to fearless. The prophetic does this in our lives too, which is why King Jehoshaphat declared, "Believe in the Lord your God, so shall you be established; believe his prophets, so shall you prosper." (v.20)

Our success in life is connected to our faith in God and our ability to discern when God is speaking through an authentic prophet. When a real prophet speaks, his words come true! (Deuteronomy 18:20-22)

Bishop Stanley M. Williams is a true prophet and I know firsthand that when he speaks, it comes to pass. So, when I was asked to write this Foreword, I gladly accepted because I know that this book will lead you to a real Word from God that will take your life to the next level.

Bishop Stan has heard from God! This prophetic Word about accelerated success will shake loose any doldrums from the economic downturn and propel you into a new season, a perpetual season of advancement and prosperity in your life. If you are tired of being in a stagnated state and desire to step out into the greatness that God has called you to, then I invite you to read this book.

Accelerated Success is not for everyone! It is only for those who will believe God and embrace this prophetic utterance. If you are really ready to release your faith and see the promises of God manifest in your life, then read on! This book is written to give you clear Biblical principles to substantiate the authenticity of this prophetic Word. Bishop Stan shows you in each chapter the Scriptural mandate behind this Word from God. Moreover, in a clear and compelling way, Bishop Stan gives basic practices to guide you on your path to success. You will not have to figure out your next faith steps because he offers them to you.

Whatever dreams and goals you have put on shelves, it's time to dust them off and expect fulfilment. Things that have taken you a long time to achieve will manifest at an accelerated speed. If you have the boldness to step out in faith you will see tangible change in your life—and it won't take long!

After all, when God gets involved, victory does not take long. When He wanted to deliver Israel from 400 years of oppression in Egypt, it didn't take Him long to lead them to freedom. When God wanted to defeat Jericho, it didn't take long to bring down the walls, even though it took decades to build them. And, if you will read this book and apply its strategies, it won't take you long to break forth into your destiny!

You can trust this prophetic Word because I have seen God perform it in Bishop Stan's life. He is living proof that the Word works! Follow his example of faith and you will walk in accelerated success in your life.

Pastor Bridget and I are so godly proud of Bishop Stan and Lady Dee Williams for taking God at His Word and standing in faith to see advancement in their own lives.

Unselfishly, they are sharing this Word with the body of Christ so that you can walk in this same grace for promotion. We have received it and encourage you to do the same. Believe it! Receive it!

Walking in Accelerated Success…

Bishop I.V. Hilliard
Senior Pastor, New Light Church
Presiding Prelate, Association of
Independent Ministries
Houston, Texas

PREFACE

It was in the Year 2012 that God gave me a prophetic word about receiving His promise of accelerated success. He said we have entered a new season where there is no more shortage because He is accelerating our success causing us to advance in the kingdom of God.

The word *acceleration* has a different meaning associated with it by different disciplines and individuals. Sports announcers will occasionally say that a person is accelerating if he/she is moving fast. Yet acceleration has nothing to do with going fast. A person can be moving very fast and still not be accelerating. Acceleration has to do with "***changing***" *how fast an object is moving*. If an object is not changing its speed, then the object is not accelerating.

Accelerated Success in the Spirit realm is when there is a shift or change caused by God's grace and favor moving on your life. Consider the Israelites and their deliverance out of the bondage they experienced in Egypt. While the Lord did take some time and sent ten plagues on the Egyptians, at the crux of the last plague, God moved quickly on their behalf. In one night they got the freedom they needed after hundreds of years in slavery. What's more, they left with jewelry and precious items that could not have been gained on their own accord! God is able!

This is a season in which the Lord is moving in the Body of Christ and bringing His faithful ones to a place of domination that they could not achieve in their own strength. It is called ACCELERATED SUCCESS.

Promotion comes from the Lord. It is not to be accounted to intelligence, looks, money, or by what the world deems success. True promotion is planned, orchestrated, and executed by the Spirit of God and activated by your obedience and faith in Him.

Finally, consider the apostle Peter, well known for having denied Christ three times. And yet he is the same man whom Jesus used to establish His church. The Apostle Peter went on to be used mightily by God to take the gospel not only to the Jews, but to the Gentiles as well.

Look not on your past but look up toward who holds your future. The Lord is working everything out for the good of those who believe in Him and are called according to His purpose. He is expanding your territory. You are moving into a good and spacious place where He will be glorified as the only true God.

Now is the time to expect incredible things. It is the year to focus on your God-given assignment. First Corinthians 2:9 tells us: *"Eye has not seen, nor ear heard, Nor have entered into the heart of man The things which God has prepared for those who love Him."* God Almighty has plans to prosper you and not to harm you, plans to give you hope and a future. His desire is to bring you into all of the goodness, grace, and prosperity of spirit, soul, and body that He has in mind for you. And in this season, He is doing a quick work.

God reveals to you what He wants to do in your life through His Spirit. It is by no accident that you have this book in your hand for the Spirit of the Lord knows the season that He is bringing you into. Get ready for your spiritual promotion. It is being manifested in the natural realm and it is here. Embrace this prophetic season in your life for the time for your Kingdom advancement is now.

INTRODUCTION

We live in a world where everything moves in an accelerated manner. Things are done much quicker today than yesterday in every aspect of society. There are ways to make computers operate faster, increase sales, income, business, and career. The key is in knowing how to advance to the next level.

God has the ability to accelerate your success. He desires to bless you and increase your resources, and bring you to the place where you are fulfilled.

ACCELERATED SUCCESS is a book that will teach you how to raise your level of expectation, because your expectation motivates you to do many things. You will learn how confession and praise are vital to the advancement of your kingdom success. Developing a new level of consciousness and learning how to negotiate out of bondage are also keys to advancing in life. But you must be willing to let go of the past and not settle for a mediocre life.

In this book, I also share how kingdom acceleration does not come without facing giants in the land. You must see beyond the wilderness, and remember that God has never lost a battle; He has never lost a fight. Through trust and faith in Jesus, our model example, you will find yourself advancing toward the Promise.

You have entered a prophetic season where God is accelerating your success. Expect Him to do incredible things in your life as you advance in His Kingdom.

PART I

A PROPHETIC SEASON OF KINGDOM ADVANCEMENT

1

CONCEPT OF KINGDOM ADVANCEMENT

What lies behind us and what lies before us are tiny matters compared to what lies within us.
—Ralph Waldo Emerson

Are you ready to be made successful by God? Perhaps this is the season for your Kingdom advancement and you did not know it. You may wonder how you can know when it is your season to succeed in an accelerated manner. When God is ready to accelerate your success, He does it in a manner that only He will get the glory.

If the time has come for God to bring you to a place of success, He often does it in an accelerated manner. To

encourage you, God sometimes uses words from the
Scriptures, or the Holy Spirit speaks directly into your
heart. He will give you insight on His divine plans or
requirements regarding a specific situation with the
expectation that you will obey Him. In most instances
your expectations are always at a level beneath the point
of God's intent and plans for your success, because His
ways far surpasses your imagination.

God has the ability to accelerate that success in your
life's experiences. His desire and plans for you are good.
He desires to bless you and increase your resources, and
bring you to the place where you are fulfilled.

A PRESENT TENSE GOD

God's Word can never be old because He is always present tense as in "right now." There's no old or new Word; it is the Word from God. He is not old or young, God is. God is eternal and He forever exists. He's not trying to begin, God is.

You must understand God being present tense, so you can believe what He says now. If you do not comprehend God now, you cannot adequately believe in his power, because you still have Him in the past while expecting something from Him in the future. He wants to advance you in this season of your life.

Hebrews 11:1 (NASB)
Now faith is the assurance of things hoped for, the conviction of things not seen.

In Hebrews 11:1, the Greek translation says "faith" is the substance. The "now" is just to draw your attention to it being present tense, which means faith is not on the way; it has already arrived.

Faith is now, it is not tomorrow or next week, it is now. Think about this; you need to put your faith in motion, otherwise something is wrong. Either you believe that the word of God is for the past or you think it is for the future. There's no way you can believe that it is right now and nothing happens when you hear it.

Heb. 12: 2

"... looking unto Jesus, the author and finisher of our faith, who for the joy that was set before Him endured the cross, despising the shame, and has sat down at the right hand of the throne of God."

In Hebrews 12:2, the time is "now" that the joy was set before Jesus, and He sat down at the right hand of the throne of God. Jesus would break that barrier so men could be saved by him giving His life, because He knew what the word was before He came.

God wants to do something in you now. He wants to do something greater with you, and He wants to accelerate your success, but your thinking must be: "God will bless me so that I can be a blessing to others." Your mind must be transformed now so His purpose can be fulfilled in your life. The time is for you to believe is now.

Think about your life today with God being present tense. After this day has ended, the past is behind you and the future is before you. As each day passes you may wonder how God remains unchanged. He cannot change; God is the same yesterday, today, and forever (Hebrew 13:8).

When you understand this you will practice living by God's Word. Undoubtedly, some of the little things and adjustments will make a tremendous difference in your life causing you to advance in the Kingdom.

Satan always tries to block the things that will cause you to get your breakthrough. He might not block you from experiencing everything else, but he will try to blind you from the one thing that you need to comprehend, and that is the concept of Kingdom advancement. If he can block you from understanding one small concept of the Kingdom, then it will certainly be easy for him to discourage you.

It may take a long time for you to see the fulfillment of God's promises in your life, but no matter how long it may take to see the fulfillment, God is faithful, He will keep His word. He is ever present at all times in all situations. His reputation is impeccable and He keeps good records.

ON TIME

One day I was listening to a highly respected leader in the Christian community when I heard him say something that made a very profound impact on me. Teaching from the Scriptures he said, "Some people come to church late but they want God to be on time." Furthermore, he added, "You know I don't sing that song: *He may not come when you want Him but He's always on time.*" He said, "He better come when I want Him, because I go when He tells me to go, I'm on time for Him.

Some people come to church late all the time, they are late for everything they do, yet they expect God to be on time." He also stated, "The Scripture clearly says in Luke 6:38 that any measure that you give is measured back to you."

I encourage you to act promptly when God speaks to you about an assignment. You know that you are late when God told you to do something three months ago and you come before Him six months later with the task unfinished.

If your assignment has a long duration, then keep working on it. If you have delayed it or have been disobedient, then repent (i.e., ask the Lord to forgive you) and move on with the task. Ask God to open your eyes so you can see the significance in obeying Him. God also speaks in future tense and He has spoken in the past. Hear what He is saying to you right now and do it.

Two critical questions you must face are as follows:

1. What is God calling me to do now, and
2. What do I need to do now?

The response to His call is obedience. Do not question everything God tells you to do. Instead, move forward with His instructions.

The key to your success in receiving the promotion that you desire is to obey God.

If you argue with God, repent immediately and get it right. There are set times, and there are moments... If God says "Leave now" and you obey His assignment, then wherever you meet "Johnny" when you arrive, that is where your assignment is on track. If you do not move promptly, but wait two hours to leave, Johnny may be gone. You cannot say you obeyed God's instructions when you know you were late.

There is no time for getting it half right. Either you do or you don't obey God in a timely manner.

Obedience must become a way-of-life for kingdom advancement.

Taking prompt action cannot be over emphasized. Do not hope for or anticipate getting a second chance if you delay in obeying the Lord. Some people have a habit of living in disobedience. They are full of being rational. Their argument is that God is merciful; they even pray asking Him to give them another chance.

I have read many stories in the Bible that describe how God dealt with certain prominent leaders and individuals. He made choices on how to deal with some persons based on His sovereign will. Some folks got another chance and some did not receive the same thing.

It seems as though God extended more mercy to some and not to others. And you say, "Well, I don't understand that." Do not try to understand it; try avoiding being caught between sides. You should aim to be on the side where God can trust you to do what He tells you to do. Never mind what others are thinking, no one can anticipate the consequences of disobedience outlined by God. Therefore, do not be disobedient.

You can change the nature of your relationship, but you cannot dictate the consequences.

You may have the power to choose to change the nature of a relationship, but you do not have the power to choose the nature of the consequences of your disobedience. Sometimes that is how people in the body of Christ approach God. They change their minds; they do whatever they want to do, even though God has already told them to do something else.

Some Christians believe that after they have repented, the consequences ought to be adjusted because they repented. Repentance does not mean an adjustment in consequences. People think it is easy, but the Bible compares a backslider to a heifer on a muddy mountain sliding backwards and unable to catch its balance. (Hosea 4:6)

Backsliders may think they are fighting the slide, so they make matters worse; some break their neck and their legs, and some fall so hard until they cannot get up again.

DESIRE TO BE A BLESSING

It is time to get focused on the Kingdom. God promised that He would accelerate your success. Now is the time to expect incredible things. It is the year to focus on your God-given assignment.

I have never asked God for anything that did not involve me being an asset to His kingdom; that is my heart's desire. I want be a blessing to the Kingdom of God.

There is a lot of selfishness imposed in our generation, and preachers have something to do with it by the way we deliver God's Word. We make you think that the only thing God is thinking about is your issue. So because He is a personal Savior, you might think your issue is most important. It may be one of the reasons why some people get angry when others do not address their issue at the time they are presented.

Some believers become upset when the pastor does not call them back or somebody from the church does not get in touch with them immediately after they call. These people forget that there are others among them who are dealing with serious issues too.

The pastor could have prayed for you, laid hands on you, counseled you seventy times, but the one time you did not get to reach the pastor or other leaders in the church, you feel that nobody cares about you or nobody loves you. It shows that the only thing that is important to you is your issue. So when God looks at people like that, He cannot count on using them to advance the Kingdom.

You must avoid living as though life is only about you. When God gets ready to accelerate you and if your perspective is not right, He cannot accelerate your success. It will be held back until you are ready to receive and can appreciate what He is doing in your life.

God wants you to advance in the Kingdom by displaying patience; running the race with endurance. Hebrews 12:1 outlines His instructions:

Hebrews 12:1
Therefore we also, since we are surrounded by so great a cloud of witnesses, let us lay aside every weight, and the sin which so easily ensnares us, and let us run with endurance the race that is set before us.

The King James and other translations use the word *"patience"* instead of endurance. The Greek meaning of *endurance* is "to bear up when in adverse circumstances." I mentioned verse 2 earlier, which tells us to *"look to Jesus as the author and finisher of our faith."* We see how Jesus did it so we can follow His example.

Verse 2 of Hebrews 12 says, "… *who for the joy that was set before him."*

Joy must be shown as you endure. Jesus endured and He had joy that was set before Him. His joy was with patience while enduring the Cross. He did not turn from it because that was His Kingdom assignment for our salvation.

"The end of your faith is about the salvation of others. It is not just about you."

I know you want to be blessed, and I know you want God to meet your needs; you want Him to do some things for you. However, you need to shift your thinking in the direction of being a blessing to others, so your testimony can bring glory to God and His Kingdom.

When you fail to succeed, ask yourself the question, "Why am I not coming into certain things, why is it that my life has not changed?" The answer is simple; you have not changed your mind about God's Word. God is speaking according to what He is providing. He knows your thoughts, and He knows where you are. But He eliminates your excuses, so you will know that He heard you when your thoughts were talking.

THE GOD OF YOUR CONSCIENCE

You want to know when God is going to bless you, He also wants to know what you want more of and for what reason. Perhaps you have not witnessed to the lost souls; you haven't talked about Him to others. You are ashamed to tell them what He has done for you. You have to talk to your conscience. That is how God does it; He speaks in our conscience. He is not walking around telling others about you; He comes right up in your conscience.

Some people are emotionally and mentally unstable, because the God of their conscience is speaking so loudly against their lifestyle. They are living up and down and cannot make good decisions, when they should have believed the Word of God; however, they never responded to it. They look for other ways to obtain satisfaction and justification without realizing their deliverance is in their obedience to ministering to others.

Those who do obey and minister to the lost are the people who will enjoy the benefits of God's Kingdom, because they advance His Kingdom. This requires moving away from the church and into taking back our territory, snatching souls out of hell. Jesus wants us to go into everyone's world. We must resort to do everything we can to reach more people for the Kingdom.

Be encouraged and empowered by the Word of God. Allow the Holy Spirit to be in you like never before. Perhaps it has been a long time since you have felt His presence. If you have felt the conviction of the Holy Spirit that means God is still with you. If there is no conviction when you hear the Word of God that means you may have fallen short. If there is no conviction that could mean the Spirit of the Lord has departed.

The way to get back to Him is to go back to the altar and repent. That is not just coming to church, which has a symbol of the altar. The altar is in your heart, and it is in your conscience, it is in your mind. So ask God for help. He wants you to succeed, and He desires to advance His kingdom through you in this season.

God wants to bless your life so that you can bless others and tell them about Him. He wants you to bring them into the knowledge of the saving power of Jesus Christ so they too can begin to raise their level of expectation for Kingdom advancement in this season.

REFLECTIONS

1. How do you benefit from God's success?

2. What are God's desires for your life?

3. How can you adapt your life to include a present tense God?

4. How have you positioned faith in your life?

5. Why should you place God in the present tense?

6. When God gives you instructions, why is it important to act now?

7. What is the importance of God accelerating your success?

8. What has God spoken into your conscience?

2

RAISING YOUR LEVEL OF EXPECTATION

Change your thoughts and you change your world.
—Norman Vincent Peale

No Word of God is devoid of power—it is only powerless when it is unspoken. There is creative power in God's spoken Word. There is also evil power present in the words of the enemy to affect and oppress everyone who speaks them. Our speech becomes shallow and empty when we respond to what the world says, speak what it says, and lose sight of what God says about our circumstances. We have to begin to expect more.

Some people don't understand that when it comes to God, they can receive what they expect, so expectation is important to receiving what God has promised. Your expectation motivates you to do many things; two key areas are: confession and praise.

CONFESSION

Confession motivates you to keep the Word in your mouth that is in agreement to what God promised you. There is power in confessing and speaking the Word of God consistently over your life. When God is in preparation for you being successful, it helps you to keep your spirit in expectation of what God has promised.

Matt. 12:34

Brood of vipers! How can you, being evil, speak good things? For out of the abundance of the heart the mouth speaks.

Your words must be in agreement with what God has promised. He said "accelerated success," so you have to speak words that are in agreement with that by saying, "God I agree with you and I thank you for it." The confession must be in your mouth. You must watch your words at all times, especially in critical times when you are trying to move forward.

Psalm 19:14

Let the words of my mouth and the meditation of my heart Be acceptable in Your sight, O Lord, my strength and my Redeemer.

Proverbs 18:21

Death and life are in the power of the tongue, And those who love it will eat its fruit.

Mark 11:23

For assuredly, I say to you, whoever says to this mountain, "Be removed and be cast into the sea," and does not doubt in his heart, but believes that those things he says will be done, he will have whatever he says.

When you start believing that your tongue has the power to bring death and life and that you can have whatever you desire if you believe it when you pray, you will pay attention to the words that come out of your mouth. "Everything you say will come to pass," includes every good and bad thing you say. So you have to pay attention to what you allow to come out of your mouth.

In Genesis chapter 3:4b, the devil spoke to Eve saying she would not die if she ate the fruit. It was not an instant death, but spiritually Adam and Eve had separated from God. Words of death will separate you from God and His promises. Always watch your words at home and in your social environment where it is easy to become relaxed among your family and friends. You might hear someone tell a lie or say something that you do not agree with, and you find that you are just going along with the casual conversation.

Sometimes there is a flow of negative talk going on in your work environment; people tend to talk about the boss or those in authority. That negative talk is affecting your spirit and you have to find a way to remove yourself from the wrong environment.

God's promises are not contingent upon the conditions of the economy. He did not say if the economy is good He will give you what you ask for. He promised to keep His word, if we will believe Him. So in a season of accelerated success, you must expect God to do what He promised.

PRAISE

Praise is important to you walking in the blessing that God promised you. It is used as a symbol of celebrating God. Praise is a symbol of what you should do at home, in your car, on the bus, in church. God resides in you; He is in your temple. You are where He lives. He is only in the building because He is with you. When you leave, He leaves.

God dwells in people not buildings made with man's hands. He is inside the hearts and minds and conscience of people. So when it comes to believing God for what He promised with accelerated success, you have to believe it with your whole heart. Repetition is important because you must speak the Word over and over until it becomes a part of your total being. Let God's praises continually be in your mouth. Raise your expectation and dare to believe He will bring your words to pass.

Hebrews 4:2
For indeed the gospel was preached to us as well as to them; but the word which they heard did not profit them, [a] not being mixed with faith in those who heard it.

Paul was dealing with the children of Israel when they heard the word preached to them. The Word of God is considered to be the gospel. When God speaks, the

Word becomes gospel. Paul says the Word did not profit them because it was not mixed with faith. Both faith and the Word are inseparable.

Romans 10:17
So then faith comes by hearing, and hearing by the word of God.

You have to hear and keep hearing in order to build your faith in the words that you hear. So hold on to your faith and remain committed to it. Work with it; focus on it and speak positive confessions at all times. Doing this is important to you reaping the benefits of success.

Unless you do what you hear, you will not get the benefits of what you hear.

You must see the joy that is set before you.

If there is no joy set before you, you will not be able to go all the way. So you have to put something in place that brings joy. It cannot be something that passes, it must be ever present. That is how you keep encouraging yourself in times of despair and disappointments. It may require hanging a picture on a wall where you can see that car or house that you desire. Sometimes you need a picture as a symbol of what you have in your mind to help you focus and fight the good fight of faith.

The devil will try to steal your joy and if he can, your goods will be stolen too. He wants you to walk in fear, compare yourself with someone else, their house, job status, anything he can put before you to get your mind engaged in the wrong direction.

God wants to expand your career, your business, take you to a higher level in the job market. You hear a voice that sounds like your own. It is a familiar voice that says you are just trying to be reasonable and make some sense out of what's going on. So you start to reason with your faith; this is something that you must never do.

Faith must be released and believed.

You cannot reason with God; you have to believe Him. Jesus had to believe when He was in that Garden. He had to believe His death on the Cross and that God would raise Him from the dead, because He had already prophesied that in three days He would rise from the grave.

THE GARDEN EXPERIENCE

Your success may require the Garden experience of discovering nobody is praying for you while you are fighting with the devil. While praying to move to the next level, you cannot afford to depend on anyone but God, because He cannot fail you. Your success comes from Him and not from the east, west, north, or south.

Wherever God is able to go, so is the devil able to go. The good news is that you have the power to choose which voice you will hear and obey. Listening to the devil will take you down little by little as he talks you out of your success. You must study the Word of God and understand the works of the devil. His reasoning always comes in the knowledge he uses with the intellect of the mind. He uses it to talk you out of your accelerated success. Do not allow the enemy to speak into your ear, seducing and deceiving you, and talking you out of your success.

God knows your end from the beginning and what you would face as you strive to advance in His Kingdom. It was His decision to accelerate your success. Believe in your heart that He desires the best for you and watch His power make the difference. Raise your level of expectation and watch miracles break forth in your life as you take on a new level of consciousness to make the right confessions and give God all the praise.

REFLECTIONS

1. In what part of your being do you hold the power of God?

2. Why is living the life of expectancy so important?

3. You want to move forward in your life. How can you accomplish this?

4. Through what area of your life can you raise your expectance of God?

5. What is the Garden Experience as it relates to your success?

3

A NEW LEVEL OF CONSCIOUSNESS

God did not have a world in mind when He created you.
He had you in mind when He created the world.
—Bishop Stanley M. Williams, Author

If you are ready to succeed in life, you must get things in order. You need to straighten out some of your business affairs and take care of whatever is possible. Do what you can with what you have, and allow God to take care of the rest. That means you should not depend on God to do the things you are supposed to be doing. You have potential that is in you and it needs to come out. When God touches you He touches your potential, so it can explode and expand. He wants to pull it out of you.

You were born and created with everything that you will ever need to fulfill your God-given purpose in life. That success is in you and if you believe in God then you must believe that He preordained and predestined your being here. The Bible says God chose you before the foundation of the world. He had you in mind when He created the world.

I want you to learn how to shift your mind to capture the Spirit of what God is saying, because it will raise your level of consciousness for an impartation to take place and move you to another level.

Ask God to give you revelation and illumination to comprehend beyond what you may have understood before or have never known. But for you to receive the impact of what I am saying, a deposit from that revelation has to be made. Once that deposit has been made, it taps the potential within you for that thing to come alive. It may not be realized immediately or over a period of time.

Breakthroughs do not come at the point of the manifestation; they come at the point of revelation. That means you can get it and nobody can take it from you. You did not receive it by accident, it was on purpose.

There must be something that you understand about God's Word or something He has done that causes you to have confidence in being different.

Hebrews 4:1-2,

Therefore, since a promise remains of entering His rest, let us fear lest any of you seem to have come short of it. 2 For indeed the gospel was preached to us as well as to them; but the word which they heard did not profit them not being mixed with faith in those who heard it."

You will gain nothing if you do not believe God's Word. But you have to keep hearing it and get it in your Spirit. The more you hear God's Word the better it is for you. Get ready for your accelerated success. God said He will accelerate you in this season so expect it now. You do not have to wait, expect it right now!

Matthew 25:14-30 tells the parable about a master who went on a journey and entrusted his three servants with his possessions. The first servant was given five talents, the second two talents, and the third one talent. The servant with five talents invested and worked with his master's money and doubled the amount. The servant who had been given two talents did the same by also doubling his master's money. The third servant who had only one talent didn't use it or invest it. Because he failed to use what his master had given him, his one talent was taken from him and given to the man who had ten talents.

This parable lets us know that God does not want to receive back merely what He has given to us. He wants us to use and multiply what He has given us. This has nothing to do with whether we have much or little but has everything to do with how we use what we have. It has everything to do with our level of consciousness.

God created man to serve Him faithfully. The Scriptures affirm this truth with the words: *"... but the just shall live by his faith."* (Habakkuk 2:4b)

We are all created with a divine purpose that is with the ability to relate to God through faith. We can all make a difference in one way or the other, but we need to realize that what we have does not really belong to us. It belongs to God. We are really only stewards of what God has given us to manage.

To say that God really owns our time, talent, and treasure is to say that He has the right to whatever He wants whenever He wants it. As the owner, He has all the rights. What we have are the responsibilities.

The Scriptures assure us that Christ will return and there will be a day of reckoning. We need to be always ready, as we do not know the time but are certain that day is coming.

There are no two people in the world with the exact same DNA. God made each one of us unique for a purpose and there is something that only you can do. God has entrusted every individual with a gift. Unfortunately, many people go through life without ever discovering their gift.

God has entrusted each of us with various resources. He is faithful and expects faithfulness. We have a choice, whether or not to submit to the Lordship of Christ. When we submit to God, He expects faithfulness from us. He expects faithfulness in our management of the resources He entrusts to us.

When God entrusts His resources into our care He expects an increase. God expects obedience to His Word. He expects a life that impacts others as we wait for His promised return.

The earth is the Lord's and all it contains and we should see ourselves as stewards of God's provisions and use every opportunity to serve Him. When we refuse to use God's provisions to serve Him, even the little we have will be taken away from us and we are left utterly useless.

The Sea of Galilee is full of life and activity and on one occasion the disciples caught so much fish that their nets were about to burst. The Jordan River flows into the Sea of Galilee, and then continues south until it flows into the Dead Sea. It is called the Dead Sea because it contains no life. No plant or animal can live in the Dead Sea. It has no life because it has no outlet. It does not use what it receives.

Are we being resourceful with what has been entrusted into our care? We all know that Jesus is coming back and we will have to account for what we did with our time, talents, and treasures.

Jesus says that He will reward us according to what we do with the resources that He has given us. Those who are faithful would be given more responsibility. When we are faithful with what God has entrusted into our care, then He will entrust even more into our care.

God owns everything and we must be careful about how we treat His possessions. The faithful ones will receive eternal joy in God's presence. The unfaithful ones will receive condemnation and will spend eternity with the weeping and gnashing of teeth in outer darkness.

We often make the mistake that the third servant made. We fail to invest what has been entrusted into our care because we feel cheated. Instead of investing what we have, we spend the time feeling sorry for ourselves, because we did not receive the same amount as others.

We can all make a difference with what we have. We cannot do everything, but we can do something. A boy once gave Jesus his meal of five loaves and two fish and this was used to feed more than 5,000 people (John 6:9-11). Jesus used what he had when the opportunity was available.

Life gives us many opportunities, to truly make a difference with our life, we must be willing to make the most of those opportunities, no matter how small they may seem.

When we develop our muscles, our reward is that we can carry heavier burdens and still feel good. To those who have, more is given. It is the same in the spiritual realm. When we act faithfully under the responsibilities that God has entrusted to us, our capacities will grow. If we do nothing with them, our ability to respond and be useful will decrease.

Jesus has given us many resources that are especially designed for us and God expects us to do something with them. We are accountable to Him as stewards of His possessions. It does not matter how small or how large those possessions are which have been entrusted to us. We are not less accountable because we have only received a little. Everyone will be asked to account for what we have done with what we received.

The world despised small things, but our Lord does not; He has given us all the resources we need to serve Him. We can, however, only serve Him when we have surrendered our lives to Him. So let us be resourceful and desire a new level of consciousness with what the Lord has given us so we can be assured of hearing Him say, "Well done, good and faithful servants!" Raising our level of consciousness will help us in knowing how to avoid being in bondage.

REFLECTIONS

1. What should God expect from you with His resources?

2. When God touches you, what is the one thing that is released within you?

3. What does the revelation of God mean to you?

4. How do you rate yourself as a steward of God?

5. How might you compare yourself to the Dead Sea?

PART II

EGYPT JOURNEY

4

NEGOTIATING OUT OF BONDAGE

God does not negotiate from bondage to wilderness, but from bondage to abundance.
—Bishop Stanley M. Williams, Author

God's Word works from the inside out, but you have to allow it to be mixed with your faith. The Old Testament Book of Exodus reveals the journey of the children of Israel in Egypt and how they knew God was going to take them from Egypt to the Promised Land, a land flowing with milk and honey, and when they came out of Egypt there was not one feeble person among them; all were wealthy.

When God brought them into the desert, He changed their diet as they were moving through. They were only supposed to be there from three weeks to a month. It was a place where they were supposed to be passing through. But they lost sight of what God told them. They did not have the faith to believe His promise.

God would never negotiate with you about getting stuck in a wilderness while you are in bondage. He does not negotiate from bondage to wilderness. Instead, He negotiates from bondage to abundance.

The Book of Exodus reveals what happened when the children of Israel cried out in Egypt. In Chapter 3 (paraphrased), Moses asked God,

"What are you going to do about these people being in bondage? It's unfair what is going on with them."

God replied: *"I have heard their cry and I have come down to deliver them."* Then Moses asked, *"Well what are you going to do about it?"*

God said *"Well I need you to go."* Moses replied, *"No, no, no, I thought You came down to deliver them."* God said: *"No, I need you to go."*

Exodus Chapter 3 shows how Moses had the burning bush experience. That was traumatizing for him, because he already had an experience with God after he was a fugitive. He had already murdered somebody and covered it up, which made him a fugitive on the back side of the wilderness. Moses saw the bush burning without being consumed. In the desert it was not unusual for a bush to be burning, but it was unusual for one to be burning and not consumed. He had the experience of God talking to him.

While you are in bondage, God talks to somebody about your deliverance.

If you've been asking God to move in your life, He will move. You just need to say, "My moment is going to come."

Once we were on our way to Houston, Texas; while sitting in the airport a young man walked up to me and said "Prophet!" We shook hands; I was cordial and asked, "Hey how are you doing?" Then he asked, "You don't remember me do you?" When he said his name I remembered; I hadn't seen him in about twenty years. So we started talking about old times. Then he started ministering and prophesying; he was accurate. While we were praying I said, "I receive that."

We sat there for a while. He waited, and I was waiting for him to go on over to his departure gate, since we had already exchanged numbers and had talked about everything. I invited him to visit my church and he was still sitting there. Now after the invitation and you have ministered to me and I received it (I normally don't let people prophesy to me), he got the red carpet, he got access. However, he remained there. Then he asked, "Do you see things getting better for me?"

He just came out and asked me. It took everything in me not to laugh. I asked, "What do you mean?" He asked, "Is the Lord showing you anything about me?" I said, "No, not in particular." He was serious as he looked at me and began asking me to tell him something. For a moment, I looked at him and I could see the look in his eyes that revealed he was having a hard time in his ministry. I asked, "Well what is it that you need?" He said, "I am on my way to preach at a church. I want to know whether this is going to be a good meeting." I said, "I don't know. Let's stand in faith and believe God that it's going to be a good meeting." He responded, "Well, is it going to be financially rewarding? Are the people going to respond?"

I explained the process that allows God to respond to us economically. I knew he had been ministering for a long time, so I asked the question: "How is your giving?" I assured him that he was on God's mind and that our time of meeting was no coincidence. He did not run into me by accident, because I am someone whose life has a purpose and God has a specific purpose. I further explained that if God allowed him to run into me at that specific time, then surely there was a purpose, and I reassured him that he was created for a specific purpose. God gave him a special assignment, just like He gave me an assignment. Since I was on my assignment by being there at that moment, then our meeting was intentional with God.

Our conversation continued as I explained how you get blessed when travelling for God. I instructed him to find someone who he could trust to sow a seed into their life, because he needed to sow his way into the next meeting when traveling. He asked, "And God will bless me financially if I do that?" I assured him that his giving would release people in the meetings to respond to an offering. God will assign people to bless him economically when he has sown into the lives of others. Whatever you sow comes back. It is the law of sowing and reaping.

Galatians 6:9

A man reaps what he sows

After giving him that revelation I noticed how his face lit up. I said, "We have an agreement that we are going to believe God will allow you to have a good meeting on this journey." I could see that he needed a good meeting. It appeared to be a deep concern to him.

Twenty years had passed since we last saw each other when we had done tent meetings together. But the point I'm making is that we met again at a time when he needed a Word from God; one that said he was going to be blessed economically. That was what he desired, but what he needed was something that would help him in not having to pray that same prayer again. He would never have to ask God and hope that his next meeting would be okay.

When you are in bondage, God talks to somebody else about your deliverance. When He wants to make you succeed, He wants to accelerate your success. You might be wondering how He is going to do it; He is talking to somebody about your deliverance.

In Exodus, God was talking to Moses while the children of Israel were struggling at their worst. They were in bondage, while God was on a mountain having a conversation with a man about their promotion. He allowed Moses to experience Pharaoh. Moses told Pharaoh: *"Let my people go."* The plagues had to go on. God had to get some glory out of that situation. He had to show that He was God. He had to let the army become the greatest army on the planet, destroy it, and then demonstrate that He was God in the sight of His people.

God brought His people out of bondage. He was leading them out and he let them go. They were walking into a place that they had never known before. He told them what He had told Abraham. God responded to that particular group of three million people. He responded to them because of the Word that He gave to Abraham.

The foundation has already been laid for your success in life and prosperity in abundance that extends to your children's children.

You must believe that it has already been done. The Israelites came out because they all wanted to be free, so they came out marching victoriously. That is how we come out too. Yes, God is with us. We come out shouting; we have the gold, and we have borrowed all the gold as we are coming out.

The wilderness is where the exchange takes place among each other. They had all the gold because they were going there to worship. They also had the cattle and everybody was walking.

Have you seen the movie *The Ten Commandments* where they were walking? Before reaching the wilderness Pharaoh came out with his choice chariots behind him. The children of Israel panicked when they saw the water in front of them and the army behind them.

This is God proving that if you are walking with Him, then He's going to prove to you on the road to success that He is with you and He's got your back. They stood facing the water while the army was behind them. Then they started complaining:

"Why would God bring us out here to kill us? Why would He get us out here and not take care of us? Why would He do this? Here is the water in front of us and the army behind us."

Before the army approached, fire separated the army from the people. They were watching the fire in the sky. That was God again. They had seen frogs and they had seen other plagues, but this time fire came down from the sky. They were watching the fire when Moses started complaining.

In Chapter 4, God asked Moses:

"What is that in your hand?"

Moses looked at it and said, *"It's a stick."*

God said. *"Use what you have and stretch it out over the water."*

He said that so they could see that they had more than enough with them to get to the place where they needed to go.

You have everything that you need to get you to your next place in destiny.

You do not need something from the outside; it is already within you.

Moses stretched the rod out and suddenly the breath of God started blowing. While it blew all night, they prepared dinner; they ate and played. They had picnics; babies were being delivered, because the Scripture said the east wind blew all night long. Fire was coming down and they watched the miracle. It was the first aquarium ever made when God made walls of water. He did that with His breath; they walked over on dry ground.

God moved all the water up so they could cross over on dry ground. There was no mud where they went across, because animals had to go across. God picked the right place because in that part of the river bed there was no bumpy or rocky road; the sand had cleared away. The ground where they walked on was only a wide piece of slate, so it was easy for them to walk across. Nobody stumbled nor fell trying to get across. After everyone had crossed over, Moses turned because the people were crying again. The chariots were coming.

Some people go from faith to fear in an instant. They do not realize that sometimes when things go wrong, it is God's plan to show the devil know he's defeated.

When the army was headed across the river they reached the center and the waters collapsed on them causing everyone to drown.

God drowns the best of devils.

He drowns poverty, lack, defeat, sickness, disease; He drowns them all.

Where are you right now? If it looks like the devil is coming toward you, let him come, God's got a trap for him. It is a sure sign that you are headed in the direction of your success. You're on your way to the Promised Land where there is no room for mediocrity.

REFLECTIONS

1. What is bondage to you?

2. How will you come out of your bondage?

3. The principles of God are available for your deliverance. What principles will you use?

4. God has cleared a path for your deliverance from bondage, so how will you walk it?

5. What do you tell the devil?

5

NO MEDIOCRITY

Who aims at excellence will be above mediocrity; who
aims at mediocrity will be far short of it.
—Burmese Saying

The Israelites reached the wilderness and settled by
the mountain and decided that they did not want to go
any further. They did not mix their faith with the Word
they heard. Instead, they started speaking things out of
fear. Their mouths got them into trouble. The things
that they spoke against were the things that God said He
would do. They began to doubt God, because they had
an environment that was mediocre instead of the one
that He promised them.

Many people miss being successful in life because they have become mediocre. They become comfortable where they are. God has so much more to give than what we ask. He expects great things from us, too.

Matthew 7:7-11 (NASB)
Ask, and it will be given to you; seek, and you will find; knock, and it will be opened to you. "For everyone who asks receives, and he who seeks finds, and to him who knocks it will be opened." Or what man is there among you who, when his son asks for a loaf, will give him a stone? Or if he asks for a fish, he will not give him a snake, will he? "If you then, being evil, know how to give good gifts to your children, how much more will your Father who is in heaven give what is good to those who ask Him!"

Do you expect God to use you? Do you expect Him to change you so you can fulfill His Kingdom purposes? Or do you just expect God to ignore you or make you do it alone?

Philippians 2:13 (NASB)
…for it is God who is at work in you, both to will and to work for His good pleasure.

The Israelites were a generation that God delivered out of bondage, but they landed in mediocrity to stay in the wilderness, rather than let God's promise take them to the Promised Land.

Someone once said, "I've never met a Christian who planned to have a mediocre life...." He never knew anyone who planned to build with wood, hay, and stubble either. He said, "I've never met a Christian who planned to have a mediocre life but I've met plenty of mediocre Christians."

Peter recognized that too, but he felt it didn't have to happen to us. Peter tells us that if we develop eight specific qualities in our lives, we will avoid being mediocre and unproductive:

"... ineffective and unproductive in your knowledge of our Lord Jesus Christ." (2 Peter 1:8)

He tells us that if we want to avoid being unproductive in our relationship with Jesus and have our Christianity count for something and mean something...then we need to: *"... add to your faith goodness; and to goodness, knowledge; and to knowledge, self-control; and to self-control, perseverance; and to perseverance, godliness; and to godliness, brotherly kindness; and to brotherly kindness, love.*

Peter says, we must start with our Faith and build on it by increasing our goodness (actions). We should strive to increase our knowledge of God and His Word. We should continually aim to control our emotions and our actions. We should stand firm and strong in difficult situations and try to imitate God in our lives; be nice to people. Learn to love others like God loves us.

It's that simple. But Peter warns us (vs. 5) that we need to *"make every effort"* to add these things to our lives. We should strive to *"possess these qualities in increasing measure"* (vs. 8).

Peter also tells us in verses 12 and 15:

I will always remind you of these things, even though you know them and are firmly established in the truth you now have….verse 15: And I will make every effort to see that after my departure you will always be able to remember these things.

Why does he stress that Christians should…make every effort to add these qualities to their lives…and that we should possess these qualities in increasing measure? Why would Peter go to such lengths to remind Christians of the importance of these "simple" qualities…even going so far as to make sure they'd remember them after his death? Why would Peter stress these "simple" qualities as if they were a life and death matter?

When people fear success they become comfortable where they are, frustrated but comfortable. They may be angry about their circumstances but that place is comfortable, livable. They begin to tolerate a mediocre life and never get to the place where they are indifferent. They never say, "This is not for me; I'm not supposed to be here. I refuse to settle for less than what God has for me."

If you are uncomfortable with where you are in life, you will experience an argument in your mind. There will be a spirit of resistance. You may experience mood swings although you might not say anything.

Someone may ask 'Hey what's wrong with you?' You quickly respond by saying, '"Nothing." Everyone around you knows something is wrong. They may repeat their question four or five times trying to get you to tell them what's wrong. But your response remains the same that you are fine; all is well. Then suddenly it comes out; you release all the frustrations about the situation that you have been tolerating.

You have to come to a place in your life when you tell yourself, "This is not the life for me; I do not want to have a mediocre life. I do not want to be bored or mediocre and not prospering. I am not afraid of taking steps of faith in moving forward in the things that God wants me to do.

This is your season of success; you no longer have the right to settle for anything less than God's promise and His Word. You cannot just sit around and say what you have is enough. No, it is not enough; God wants you to have more. It is not just about you and your fall any more. God needs you to be in a position where you can be a blessing to somebody else.

If you do not get delivered, how you can you help somebody else be delivered? If you do not have anything, how are you going to be able to give something to somebody else? They were stuck there and God came down to judge the generation.

God told Moses He was going to wipe out that generation and raise another one. Moses reminded God that because it had gone out in all the lands that He was going to take them to the Promised Land. If that did not happen, the people would say God was not able.

God asked what they were going to do there, because He was ready to kill all of them. They were ready to stone Moses earlier, and God came down and stepped between them threatening to kill everyone. He was between the people and God and told them to stop and get back in faith, while he asked God to cease from killing them.

There was doubt and fear while pleading for another revelation that they could be left behind. Moses argued and negotiated.

God will skip over you and choose somebody else, especially after He has been pleading for you to get in line and move forward.

It may mean finding someone out of wedlock, the rejected stone, a David. He will raise him up.

Moses was told that their lives would be spared, but they were not going into the Promised Land. They were going to stay in the wilderness and die. That was the word they spoke over themselves, so they would live and die by their word, except for the younger generation that was ages twenty and under. This experience came after they knew the land was flowing with milk and honey. They had sent spies over there, and they had physical proof that the land had in it what God had promised. They had seen the glory and came back testifying how the land was flowing with milk and honey.

How do we know God is great? We have seen what He has done for others. It is our confession of being too insignificant, like grasshoppers. They started having grasshopper mentality like they had done previously. They also had a lot of time to think and relax with no conflict going on in the wilderness; there was no resistance to anything.

It is easy to sit around and get manna from the sky, and just eat and have your clothes grow. You do not even need to go shopping because your clothes are growing on you. You also have protection; a hedge around you, a cloud by day and a pillar of fire by night to keep warm.

You might think it is easy to talk about what you are not going to do and how independent you are; you have your own mind that says you can do whatever you want to do.

If you believe you can do what you want to do, then you have forgotten that it is about doing God's will for your life. You have been bought with a price; you have been purchased from the enemy, sin, death, and sickness. He bought you, which means He owns you. It is about you doing what the Lord tells you to do. He wants to lift you out of the life of mediocrity. Learn to think bigger, expect greater, and know that your accelerated success is coming, because you have passed the experience test.

REFLECTIONS

1. Do you think there is mediocrity in the kingdom of God?

2. How will you build on your relationship with God?

3. When does fear play a part in mediocrity?

4. What would challenge you to become uncomfortable with your state of mediocrity?

5. You are owned by God, so how would you bring Him glory in your situation?

6

THE EXPERIENCE TEST

Experience is the child of thought,
and thought is the child of action.
—Benjamin Disraeli

The Book of Numbers Chapter 13 records the wilderness journey of Twelve Spies, one from each of the Twelve Tribes dispatched by Moses to scout out the Land of Canaan for 40 days as a future home for the Israelites. This would be the beginning of their faith journey from bondage in the desert of Egypt to the land of Canaan that God promised Abraham through his son, Isaac.

There are many things that happen to test our faith when moving toward the promise that God has for us. Maintaining full trust in Him is an area where many people are challenged, especially if they have never had to go through a faith test.

The Israelites were about to be delivered from bondage to a place of prosperity. That is the time that people should be jumping up and down celebrating because God has spoken. They should be shouting all the way through, because they have seen Him perform miracles in their midst.

God allowed the Israelites to see some amazing things to give them a testimony about their deliverance from bondage. Their deliverance may be in the area of finances, and they suddenly find themselves with more money than they have ever had. So they are coming out loaded after having been broke all their lives. The problem is that they do not know how to manage what they have. Every time someone calls them with a need, they take care of it.

People will tell you not to worry because they have much more to share. That is the movement from bondage to the wilderness. Some people go through their wilderness experience having the joy of being fed by God every time they have a need like the Children of Israel received miracle after miracle from God.

God is always there to take care of His children. It is like people who live on a fixed income but they always have more than enough every day. Somehow God always worked things out for them. They see His mighty hand working on their behalf. The manna always shows up just in time for their next meal. Soon they reach a daily comfort zone.

WILDERNESS NEVER A PROMISE

The wilderness and the manna were never a promise from God. He did it because it was needed where they were passing through the wilderness. God did not promise to clothe the Israelites, because they were supposed to be passing through the wilderness rather than staying there. Their clothes were not supposed to grow on them. Everyday they woke up and looked outside and found manna, food, bread, honey, and wheat falling from the sky. They did not have to be concerned about anything coming up from the ground to feed them. Each new day was a reminder of God's glory coming while they were in the wilderness.

NO FIGHTING EXPERIENCE

When it is time for people to move forward, they enter a new dilemma especially when they have no fighting experience on their résumé. The Israelites had never been in a war; there was never a fight. They never had to take anything by force.

We know some people like that today called Christians. Some do not know how to handle anything because they have never had to fight their way through a situation to possess their land. Just because God is with you does not mean you are not going to be in a fight. Jesus promised to never leave us nor forsake us. But He did not say we would live a carefree life without trials and tribulations.

Everyone should learn how to fight.

If I know that I am about to engage in a fight, I will ask my congregation whether they are with me. That does not mean that I do not need to fight. I know that they are expecting me to enter the ring first. I cannot stand on the sideline and expect them to enter the battle when I should be leading the way.

Moses chose twelve men, one out of every tribe to go and examine the land of Canaan. He gave specific instructions for their arrival at a place called Eshcol. They were told to cut down a branch with a cluster of grapes and bring them back as proof for what God had promised in the land He promised them. After forty days they returned to Paran to show Moses and the people the fruit they had brought with them, and to acknowledge that the land was fertile.

The Israelites did return with physical proof, so there was no way they could deny the truth about the land having what God promised. However, when they saw those giants in the land, they could not see themselves entering a fight with those guys.

Never doubt the generational blessing that God has already prepared for you.

Prior to seeing giants for the first time, ten of the leaders were sure about God keeping His word. Suddenly, their perspective changed and they concluded that God was not capable of honoring His promise. They had no proof, only that the giants were bigger and taller than anyone among their camp.

Their experiences testify to their ability to succeed, but in the face of fear, they could not see beyond what they knew. Something happened to them within those forty days in the land among giants. They no longer believed in God, and surely they did not believe in themselves.

Never try to figure out who God will use to bless you.

Something supernatural was happening while these leaders were challenged with their belief when they reached the wilderness to possess the land prepared for them. They saw different people who had prepared that land for them. The Israelites could not believe their eyes when they saw giants overseeing land that was flowing with milk and honey. The harvest was great and the ground was yielding plentiful, far beyond measure.

A cluster of grapes was huge and heavy. The men had to bring them back on a pole over their shoulders. It did not matter how large or small the men were; they could not carry those grapes alone, because each grape was the size of a grapefruit.

There is a place in Africa where someone taught the people the principle of giving and prosperity, so they began to sow in the ground where they were taught the Word of God. The sowing has resulted in unusually large produce. They are harvesting organic fruits and vegeta-

bles that look abnormal compared to the regular size we
see in America.

**Your success already exists; God is not trying to
create it.**

God has already prepared things for you that you have
yet to discover such as your success. It already exists;
God is not trying to create it. Anything that God reveals
to you is a finished product. He does not speak until
He's finished. That is the reason for Him being sure.
When He starts talking to you about your next success
and how He's going to bless you, move your life forward,
it means He has already set those things in motion.

You must have the proper perspective.

Moses sent twelve men to examine land that was
already flowing with milk and honey. Joshua and Caleb
were the only two who had the proper perspective about
the situation after looking at the fertile land and seeing
the giants who were the caretakers.

These two leaders had a perspective that said they
were well able to possess what they saw. The other ten
men could not see things with the proper perspective;
they weren't thinking about Israel and how the children

had just come out of bondage. They were in the wilderness observing giants walking with a stick. There were Canaanites and the Hittites, people of war who had been fighting since they were young.

In fact, ten of the twelve leaders had never been in a fight, no war experience, yet they believed in the only true living God. Their report was that they saw themselves like grasshoppers compared to those giants.

WRONG PERSPECTIVE

The Israelites had the wrong perspective about the giants after having spent forty years of bondage in Egypt. They had no experience with other cultures and communities. So they did not know that those other kind of people and that tall structures existed in the world. Some had heard the stories but seeing them with their own eyes was phenomenal.

When they returned after forty days of searching out the land flowing with milk and honey, they had a "but" or "nevertheless" (KJV) moment. You will always find those kinds of people who cannot give a full positive report. There is always negative talk that starts with "but" or "nevertheless."

Report on the Exploration:

Numbers 13:28-30
But the people who live there are powerful, and the cities are fortified and very large. We even saw descendants of Anak there. 29 The Amalekites live in the Negev; the Hittites, Jebusites and Amorites live in the hill country; and the Canaanites live near the sea and along the Jordan.

Then Caleb silenced the people before Moses and said,

30 *We should go up and take possession of the land, for we can certainly do it.*

Although God tells people what they are capable of achieving, there are still some who will say "but" or "nevertheless" as though they have never seen miracles. Imagine God has already shown you the promise and you spend forty days enjoying it then you tell God you are not ready to possess it.

God has never lost a battle.

God gave His children all that land as an inheritance, but they still found it difficult to believe they were capable of overtaking the people. Sadly, they had the wrong perspective, which caused them to believe the giants were actually physically stronger and of a much greater sizes in statue.

Numbers 13:31-33

But the men who had gone up with him said, "We can't attack those people; they are stronger than we are." 32 And they spread among the Israelites a bad report about the land they had explored. They said, "The land we explored devours those living in it. All the people we saw there are of great size. 33 We saw the Nephilim there (the descendants of Anak come from the Nephilim). We seemed like grass-hoppers in our own eyes, and we looked the same to them.

There has never been a man whose arms were long enough to box with God, and there has never been a man capable of winning a fight with God. His track record speaks for itself. Knowing the facts helps us in making right decisions surrounding our circumstances. We must know the source of our information; God cannot lie. His life is an open book.

God has never lost a fight.

God has never lost a fight, not even when He was in heaven and Lucifer said he was going to take over heaven with his own splendor and glory. God did not respond to Lucifer, He just told Michael and his angels to take care of Lucifer. They kicked him out of heaven.

God does not lose; He cannot fail and He does not lie.

I pray that you will walk in the promise of success in your life. That means you must be willing to be totally transformed by the power of Jesus Christ.

Decide now to trust God like you have never trusted Him before.

Make a commitment to keep your word and do what He tells you to do, because this is your season for accelerated success.

Believe God's Word, receive it, and walk in it.

Do not allow anyone to hinder you from experiencing your success now.

Remember the battle belongs to the one who has never lost a battle; He has never lost a fight. His track record is perfect.

Now is the time for you to set your sight on entering the race that is set before you and be determined to run it with patience, enduring every roadblock, and allowing every stumbling block to become a stepping stone that will allow you to advance in your Kingdom assignment.

REFLECTIONS

1. If you have ever encountered a wilderness experience, what is your deliverance testimony?

2. Give an example of how God reacts while you are passing through the wilderness?

3. When you go beyond what you see, how do you trust God?

PART III

RESETTING YOUR FOCUS

7

RUN WITH PATIENCE

No road is too long for him who advances slowly and does
not hurry, and no attainment is beyond his reach who
equips himself with patience to achieve it.
—Jean de La Bruyère

Resetting our focus to achieve our accelerated success requires us to run the race with patience. When God wants to do something great in and through us, we have to be careful not to force things to happen too soon. Sometimes we have to wait for God's timing to make it happen, because we do not want to rush God. It is not that He is against us desiring to achieve our success in an accelerated manner, but it could be that He wants to make sure we are fully equipped to handle certain situations and events that He knows will be on our pathway.

King David was anointed by the prophet Samuel to one day be the future king of the nation of Israel (I Samuel 16:13). There was already a king over the nation of Israel when David was anointed. But God started preparing him for his accelerated success.

In the beginning David killed the giant Goliath and everyone rejoiced (Ch. 17). His patience was tested in being a sheepherder and having to fight wild animals while waiting for his accelerated success. But he endured the challenges and was promoted to being a General in King Saul's army, and God led him from one victory to another.

David's patience kept him in the right place at the right time, and the enemy was defeated time and time again. There was nothing ordinary about the way God was preparing him for his future job. But he had to learn not only how to handle success as God prepared him to become the king, he also had to learn how to handle defeat as God continued to prepare him for his throne.

SUCCESS AND DISAPPOINTMENTS

Your accelerated success will require you to know how to handle success and disappointments. Some people will be happy to see you rise to the top and there will be those who will say, "Who do you think you are?" David's quick rise to the top made King Saul nervous (Ch. 18), the King heard the women singing;

Saul has slain his thousands, and David his tens of thousands. (v. 7)

The king became very upset and jealous. He made up his mind that he would have to get rid of David. At first he tried killing him by sending him into battles he did not think David could possibly win. Then Saul tried killing David by throwing a spear at him. He did not stop there, his tactics just changed by sending others to find David. Finally, Saul tried to kill David by going after him with 3,000 men.

When David heard the good news of becoming the king one day, he did not know that part of the lesson would include personal and live training sessions on how to avoid assassination attempts on your life. We learn many of the lessons in preparing to become the person God wants us to become in real life situations.

One of the reasons God had David out there in the wilderness was to learn how to survive when a more powerful enemy is pursuing you to take your life. God had not forgotten David in the desert. He was preparing David for the things that would come in his accelerated success.

Twenty five years after David became king, somebody was chasing him to kill him in the desert, and what David was learning would help him to survive. That is why we need to run our race with patience rather than going through hard times complaining. God is equipping you for something that you do not know about that is in your destiny.

FORGET ABOUT YOUR ENEMIES

David decided to forget about Saul and go on with his life. He found this beautiful woman by the name of Abigail and took her as his wife. No sooner than the two of them got together, and before they could celebrate their honeymoon, the Ziphites again went and told Saul, "King Saul, if you still want to get David, we know where he is." So in Chapter 24, Saul was all forgiving. But by Chapter 26 things had changed.

King Saul's hatred had the time to be stirred up again, so once again with his special private army of 3,000 choice soldiers, he went after David. At first David could not believe that the king was coming after him again. He said,

"God we have already gone through this, what is the problem? Didn't you see what I did the last time he approached me. God you have got to cut me some slack somewhere."

David sent some spies to make sure Saul was definitely coming after him. Upon their return to the camp, the men said,

"Oh yes brother, he is definitely coming after you."
David said, "Man I have to go see this thing for myself.
There has to be a mistake."

Sometimes there is a mistake, but the mistake is on us.
David felt, he had already demonstrated his willingness
to not take matters in his own hand to become the king.

**Your test of patience in an area last week or last
month does not mean you are going to easily con-
quer that area the next time it comes up.**

What area are you facing today that makes you feel
deep within that you are rushing, because you don't
believe that God is moving fast enough in making it
happen for you? Are you compromising even though
you know it is not the right thing to do? If you want to
stay in God's perfect will, then you must remember that
His timing is everything.

PATIENCE AND TEMPTATION

There are plenty of opportunities that are going to come your way, but it may not be God's will for you to take some of them. Many will come as a test of your patience, others as a temptation. You may think that you cannot pass up this opportunity. If you take the opportunity, it will draw you closer to God. Will you be sacrificing your family because there is no time or energy left to share with them? Will you be selling a little piece of your soul because of compromises? If something is of God, He does not require you to sacrifice part of your relationship.

Sometimes we think about things that are convenient rather than best suited for us. Christians will often pledge their allegiance to Christ, but when they get an opportunity to obtain something that they really want, they will sacrifice in the name of "I might not get this opportunity again."

Often when we have a goal, we want to reach it as soon as possible. We often think that pain means we need to change our goal, but sometimes a willingness to accept pain demonstrates our commitment to the goal. We look at our lives and deceive ourselves into thinking, "I must have all this now. But that's not usually God's way.

In Matthew 6:11, Jesus taught his disciples to pray, *"Lord give us today, our daily bread."*

We would rather God give us today's bread, tomorrow's bread, and all the bread we need for the next twenty years right now." No God has some bread in his timing for us today and some different bread for us tomorrow. Our problem is that we cannot see where the bread for tomorrow is coming from.

David had to have been tempted to just go and take matters into his own hands. After all, there was this opportunity and it probably would not come again. Do not listen to others tell you what a great opportunity you're about to miss. I've seen many a great opportunity lead people right out of their relationship with God. They pursue material wealth, name recognition, and the desire to be loved. All can be deadly opportunities for our spiritual lives. God has a time set for all of these things for our lives. If we are faithful to Him, he says He will give us the desires of our hearts.

David chose to believe that if God had anointed him king then God was able to make him king without him compromising his faith. So what if he would have to wait a little longer in that miserable desert. It could mean a smaller paycheck or a smaller house. You must value your relationship and integrity with God and allow it to be demonstrated in your life.

Everyone faces different circumstances and trials. Your trial is not my trial and mine is not yours, but rest assured, there are some Christians somewhere who are going through the same dilemma as you are.

In 1 Peter Chapter One, Peter says you should not be surprised at the painful trial that you are suffering, as though something strange was happening to you. (1 Peter 4:12)

God knows what you're going through. He has already seen you coming out, moving up and achieving your accelerated success. Ask yourself the following questions:

Will doing this draw me closer to God?

Will doing this make my family a better family in terms of its relationships?

Will choosing this path bring me more into the life of the church?

Will making this choice make me more in the image of Jesus Christ?

There is a time for God to provide us with what we need and what He has promised us. Satan always tries to make us have it all right now. God's way is always best. So run your race with patience and set a mark so you do not allow anything to steal your joy.

REFLECTIONS

1. Why is it important to wait on God's timing?

2. While waiting for your accelerated success, what has been your test?

3. How have you learned patience?

4. Knowing God provides opportunities for you, why is it important to wait for them?

5. Why is "now" not always the best time for you to receive your accelerated success?

8

SET A JOY MARKER

Our plans miscarry because they have no aim.
When a man does not know what harbor he is making for,
no wind is the right wind.
—Seneca

Now that you have been able to reset your focus to achieve your accelerated success, you need to set a joy marker that will help you in staying focused. You must grab hold of the joy that is set before you and never let it go. You have to choose to hold onto it, because joy will keep you from getting discouraged.

God must always be with you on the journey. He is the key player. When you do not think He has you on

His mind, He's holding you up never to let you fall. When you do not feel anybody else is thinking about you, God has already been talking to people about you. That is why you need the joy set before you. It is not your job to think about who God is going to use because it is His job.

This is important for you to know, because God wants to make you succeed, but He's got to get you in a place where you are led by the Spirit and not by your flesh. You cannot be led by head knowledge or information given by familiar spirits. When you are led by the Spirit instead of those things, you will always find joy. It is your marker for taking the journey with God.

Many times things may be absent from your mind about how you are going to reach your destiny. You cannot figure out how God is going to get you there, how something is going to happen. Thoughts will try to bombard your mind to make you depressed because the enemy wants you to feel overwhelmed, like you are going to have a mental breakdown. You may even feel it is your job to figure out who God should use to get you to where He has promised you. Your mind cannot handle that, but it can handle the joy that is set before you.

Heb. 12:1-3

Therefore, since we are surrounded by such a great cloud of witnesses, let us throw off everything that hinders and the sin that so easily entangles. And let us run with perseverance the race marked out for us, 2 fixing our eyes on Jesus, the pioneer and perfecter of faith. For the joy set before him he endured the cross, scorning its shame, and sat down at the right hand of the throne of God. 3 Consider him who endured such opposition from sinners, so that you will not grow weary and lose heart.

Your job is to keep the joy that is set before you. That means having a picture of where you are going. Do you know what you want, what makes you happy? I have learned that there are different things that make some people happy; things that they really enjoy.

People have an expectation based on what they see in someone else. I learned at a young age to never do that, because you may end up with something that someone else has without the joy. If that was never something that God wanted you to have and you went after it, then you will surely have it but misery will also come with it instead of joy. You will find yourself letting go of it because of the misery that it brings into your life.

You may have something that others did not receive because of your environment being stable and good for you. It may have been the right kind of home, with the right morals and values being imparted into your life at an early age.

Perhaps you did not appreciate what you had, but there were others looking on from the outside wishing their family life was as stable as yours. They dream that one day they would wake up and find peace and soundness of mind in their family. So when God gives it to them, you can see their joy and feel happy for them. Some people will not be happy; instead they will start comparing themselves with someone else.

I feel blessed to have the greatest joys in the world when I think about the family that God has given me. I have a wife and children who love God; I am the pastor of a wonderful church. I obey God in doing the things that He has designed for me. Yet none of them surpass what God has given me, none of what my expectations are, because of the joy that was set before me. I am walking in that joy.

There are people who do not share the same things in their life and they feel they need more than what I have to experience joy. They want more than a wife and family who are serving God. Their resentment shows in the way they address the issue. You might wonder why they are angry and not experiencing the joy that is set before them. If I am happy driving a pickup truck, then you should not become upset when you see that I am enjoying the things that God gave me or has called me to do.

The joy that is set before you is what will help you to stay on course. No person will be able to distract you and make you lose your focus if you have your joy marker. Jesus is the Author and Finisher of your faith. You do not need to worry about someone else when you have joy, and be careful about who you talk to because you cannot satisfy other people.

Some people will always question everything they see you doing to achieve your accelerated success. It is okay to stay away from those kinds of people. Nothing will ever satisfy them and they aren't happy until they see you join them in their misery party. You should run from them, because they will question everything that you do and cause you to lose track of your own joy marker.

Joy motivates faithfulness.

1 Corinthians 15:58

Therefore, my dear brothers and sisters, stand firm. Let nothing move you. Always give yourselves fully to the work of the Lord, because you know that your labor in the Lord is not in vain.

Be steadfast.

It is in view of the joy set before us that Paul exhorts us to be steadfast, unmovable, always abounding in the work of the Lord. Paul has just set before them convincing assurances of the future resurrection. In view of these assurances they ought to remain faithful to the Lord, firm and unmoved within themselves regarding the position they had taken, giving no room to doubts and wavering (Hebrews 10:23; James 1:6).

Be unmovable.

The same assurances make us unmovable or unshakeable from outside influences. Our assurance is so sure that no one can shake us from our convictions (2 Timothy 2:16-18; 2 Thessalonians 2:2; I Timothy 1:19-20).

Always abounding in the work of the Lord.

a. The work—Spreading the gospel, helping the afflicted, and all that the Lord has prepared for us to do (1 Timothy 6:17-18; Titus 2:14; 3:8, 14; Hebrews 13:21)

b. Abounding—We are to do as much as we can, even to excess (Colossians 2:7; 1 Thessalonians 4:1; 2 Thessalonians 1:3)

c. Always—Christians are never to slack but to always be engaged in the work of the Lord (Galatians 4:18; Colossians 4:12; 1 Peter 3:15)

It is because of our faithfulness that Jesus will welcome us into the joy of the Lord (Matthew 25:21).

Joy causes us to purify ourselves.
(1 John 3:1-3; 2 Peter 3:11, 14)

If we fail to purify ourselves, we shall not see God (Hebrews 12:14; Matthew 5:8). Jesus is set before us as the model of purity. (1 John 3:3; 1 Peter 1:16)

1. He had no sin within. (1 John 3:5)

2. He was without sin. (Hebrews 4:15)

3. He knew no sin. (2 Corinthians 5:21)

4. He did no sin. (1 Peter 2:22)

Having great and precious promises set before us, we are to cleanse ourselves of all filthiness (2 Corinthians 7:1) of the flesh and the mind.

1. **Flesh**—outward sins: adultery, fornication, murders, drunkenness, reveling, etc. (See Galatians 5:19-21)
2. **Mind**—all inward sins: idolatry, lasciviousness, hatred, envying, etc. (See Galatians 5:19-21)

Joy enables us to endure hardships.
(Hebrews 12:1-3)

a. God has not said we shall be free of hardships, in fact, there are several warnings of such.
(1 Peter 4:1; 2 Timothy 3:12)

b. But as we, imitating Jesus, set our minds and hearts on the hope and joy that is set before us, we are able to endure all hardships. (1 Peter 4:13; Luke 6:22-23)

We have now considered the hope and joy set before us. If you are a Christian and you are not experiencing that joy then perhaps you need to study this subject more closely, because it is essential to remain faithful, pursue purity, and endure hardship. This is the anchor for maintaining your joy marker as you reset your focus in the direction of the accelerated success that God wants you to have now. If you are not a Christian then you are urged to come to Jesus and begin experiencing that joy today.

Say this prayer aloud now:

Heavenly Father, I come to you as a sinner asking you to forgive me of all my sins, as I invite Jesus into my heart and confess Him as Lord over my life from this day forward.

REFLECTIONS

1. At what position will you place your joy and why?

2. What are some of the consequences of placing yourself in another person's position of joy?

3. Someone is having a pity party, will you accept that invitation? Explain why/why not.

4. What do you experience when you have the joy of the Lord?

5. How does the work of the Lord relate to you having joy?

9

Our Model Example

*Ask and it will be given to you; search, and you will find;
knock and the door will be opened for you.*
—Jesus

Often we pause in life to reset our goals, and we aim to fulfill them without having a model example. Many great leaders from all walks of life have set the pace before us, but there is one who is the greatest of all. He is Jesus Christ our Lord and Savior. We are to be like him and imitate his life. He tells us this:

I have set you an example that you should do as I have done for you. (John 13:15)

Jesus Christ has become our example in countless ways, but I want to focus on three. The first one is as follows:

Jesus is the perfect example of self-sacrifice.

Many of the firemen who rushed into the burning World Trade Center in New York on September 11, 2001, understood that they were not only risking their lives but would probably die trying to rescue the innocent victims. It was the ultimate sacrifice.

Jesus died not only for the deserving, but the undeserving too. He died for those who loved him and hated him.

Romans 5:6-8
You see, at just the right time, when we were still powerless, Christ died for the ungodly. 7 Very rarely will anyone die for a righteous person, though for a good person someone might possibly dare to die. 8 But God demonstrates his own love for us in this: While we were still sinners, Christ died for us.

He sacrificed himself for those who cared and for those who could care less. Jesus had real concern for real people. There was nothing fake or pretentious about his love or concern. This love of his for us would cost him everything. He willingly gave up his place in glory to come to earth and subject his own self to the limitations of a human body.

Jesus exposed himself to hate and hunger, thirst and temptation, suspicion and rejection, torture and a terrible death. They called him a devil and a liar. They ignored his miracles and the good he did, and criticized his methods. They picked up rocks to stone him. They spit on him as he died. All of this so you would have a Savior. There was not a word of self-pity from him. In fact, he laid down the challenge for us to follow his example of self-sacrifice when he said,

Luke 14:33
In the same way, any of you who does not give up everything he has cannot be my disciple.

He said, *"If anyone would come after me, he must deny himself and take up his cross and follow me."*
(Matthew 16:24)

This is the ultimate challenge. The problem with having Jesus as an example is that it means we are supposed to follow his example.

We are to live self-sacrificing lives.

We are to live free of self-pity and live courageously.

After Christ's death and resurrection, he came to Peter and described to him the kind of death with which he would glorify God. Then he said to him,
"Follow me!" (John 21:19).

Jesus had already gone before Peter and set the example. And now Peter knew that he was called to follow Jesus' example of sacrifice and courage. And this is the important second point:

Jesus is the perfect example of courage.

I am not sure what kind of courage it takes to walk up the stairs of a burning building knowing there might not be a way out, and I am not sure I have that kind of courage. I do not know what kind of courage it took to walk up Calvary's hill, knowing there was a way out, but determined not to take it.

What kind of courage would it take to ride into Jerusalem and know that some of the same crowd that was yelling *"Hosanna"* today would yell *"Crucify"* tomorrow?

Just how much did we mean to him, for him to endure the shame and suffering of the cross, and then be separated from the Father as he became a sin offering for us? I know I don't have that kind of courage.

I know that our Perfect Example expects us to follow His example. He invites us to deny ourselves, take up our cross, and follow him.

Heb. 12:2-4

Let us fix our eyes on Jesus, the author and perfecter of our faith, who for the joy set before him endured the cross, scorning its shame, and sat down at the right hand of the throne of God. Consider him who endured such opposition from sinful men, so that you will not grow weary and lose heart. In your struggle against sin, you have not yet resisted to the point of shedding your blood.

Historically some people have taken the challenge and followed Christ even to death. There are people all around the world who have enormous courage as they face suffering and even face death because of their faith.

There are daily reports of suicide bombers who are willing to give their lives in order to kill people they see as evil. It is still hard to imagine how the terrorists on September 11, 2001, were willing to fly those planes into the World Trade Center Towers knowing they would kill themselves in an act of hatred.

Some people are willing to die for a cause like that when so many Christians are afraid to let it be known that they are followers of Christ. Jesus was willing to die for us, and he asks that we be willing to live for him. We need to have the courage to dare to be different.

We must have courage if we are going to follow Christ. That means being willing to stand up and be counted.

We have to follow Christ when everyone else is going in a different direction.

We need to be the kind of person the devil considers to be a dangerous Christian.

We have to be willing to follow even if it costs us something. Anyone can follow the ways of the world, but if you want to be a true rebel, follow Jesus.

We must be like the apostle Paul who, when he reached the end of his difficult life, said,

2 Timothy 4:7-8

I have fought the good fight, I have finished the race, I have kept the faith.

He finished by saying,

"Now there is in store for me the crown of righteousness, which the Lord, the righteous Judge, will award to me on that day—and not only to me, but also to all who have longed for his appearing."

We must face life with courage that springs from faith in a God who cares for us.

THE PERFECT EXAMPLE OF LOVE

Jesus did not come to us out of a sense of duty, or even pity. He came to us with a love burning in his heart for us. He was not thinking about what he had to give up, he was thinking about what he could give. He was not thinking about his sacrifice, he was thinking about saving us. What causes people like the firemen to rush into a burning building? For some it is a sense of duty, for others it is a sense of adventure and a love for the job, still others are driven by a love for people and a desire to help. For Jesus, love was the motivating factor. Is it any wonder that the best loved words in Scripture are the following?

John 3:16-17

For God so loved the world that he gave his one and only Son, that whoever believes in him shall not perish but have eternal life. For God did not send his Son into the world to condemn the world, but to save the world through him.

This is the example of love we are called to follow.

I Peter 2:21-23

To this you were called, because Christ suffered for you, leaving you an example that you should follow in his steps. "He committed no sin, and no deceit was found in his mouth." When they hurled their insults at him, he did not retaliate; when he suffered, he made no threats. Instead, he entrusted himself to him who judges justly.

Love overlooks the insult and injury because it looks to God and not to the circumstances. Love overcomes obstacles and looks for ways to serve and bless. Christ has called us to follow his example, for he has said,

John 15:12-13
My command is this: Love each other as I have loved you. Greater love has no one than this, that he lay down his life for his friends.

Following Christ is not an easy task, and neither was it easy for Christ to give us his life example. He never promised us that the road would be easy.

Luke 22:42-44
"Father, if you are willing, take this cup from me; yet not my will, but yours be done." 43 An angel from heaven appeared to him and strengthened him. 44 And being in anguish, he prayed more earnestly, and his sweat was like drops of blood falling to the ground.

Think about the sacrifices others have made for you. Consider how you could make sacrifices for others that would be the best example of our model Leader. People need to see how you go through your wilderness experience so they can know Christ by your life.

REFLECTIONS

1. In order for you to model your life after Jesus, what must happen?

2. How would you accomplish the sacrificial task of taking up the cross of Christ to follow Him?

3. How do you cultivate courage?

4. What motivates you to demonstrate your love toward others?

10

SEE BEYOND THE WILDERNESS

You can never cross the ocean until you have the courage to lose sight of the shore.
—Christopher Columbus

If you are not willing to focus on your accelerated success, you are not going to get there. The devil will keep you distracted with all kinds of thoughts. It is too much to be dwelling over how this person thinks, what that other person thinks, what another person is thinking about, or what might they be thinking about, that is too much thinking. You should not be thinking about that at all and wondering whether people are going to like you or not be favorable toward you.

If you occupy your mind with this kind of thinking, you will begin to look at people in a strange light; next your mind will become distracted. You begin to think, what is this person saying? So now because of all this you go to bed worried about what somebody else could be thinking about you when they are probably sleeping, which is what you should be doing.

WRONG THOUGHTS—BAD RESULTS

When you go to bed thinking about these kinds of things, you dream about them, and wake up with your mind made up that something did not happen for you because this or that person didn't like you. All of a sudden you start agreeing with these thoughts in your mind. You start judging yourself to the point of not being able to clearly see the real picture.

Next you become distracted and your own self image becomes degraded. In one day you go from the top of the mountain to the lowest part of the valley. You have engaged yourself in what other people are thinking about you.

So you no longer have the ability to focus, you view yourself in a completely different light. You're not talking about it, you're coming out as you did before, but in your mind you are carrying a heavy load. You become depressed and people don't even know that you are depressed because you're acting as if everything is all right. But mentally you have jumped off the cliff. You have committed suicide from where you were.

From that moment to the next moment a slow change starts to take place. You slowly start getting discouraged; slowly you stop moving toward the goal. Slowly, you start to hope things come around and hope things happen. Now you've moved from faith to hope. You are no longer actively participating in accomplishing what God promised you. Instead of believing through, you do not see the evidence, you say, "Well I just don't understand why it's like this with me." Stop listening to all these people.

BECOME ACCOUNTABLE

A Pastor and I may be having a conversation and one of us hears the other say something that carries a negative tone, we will immediately bring correction. One of us will say, "Oh no, we're not going down there, I'm not even going to think about that. The devil is a liar." Then we start rebuking the devil, because that's what he will do. His job is to take control of your mind so you can engage in negative thoughts that you feel people are thinking about you.

When I hear what people say about me sometimes I am shocked. Really, I am in shock, and I wonder how they ever arrived at that conclusion, especially when I know I have never met them. I've never even talked to them; don't even remember ever laying eyes on them. In complete view, somebody has said something and by the time you get down the line, the information has changed. So you get all this stuff in your head and it gets you distracted, because the mind is the battle ground.

NO ROOM FOR A PITY PARTY

Why are we so surprised when our vision constantly trips us up? We tend to take a look around and focus on the wrong things, and as we do so, that tends to bring us down. We start to develop our own little pity party—why aren't things going my why? Why does so and so get everything they want? Why do bad, sinful people get to do so much, and here I am stuck with nothing? Why do I never get the breaks in life? Why is it that bad things always come into my life?

In life when we don't pay attention to certain things, it ends up costing us also. We must be alert; we must pay attention to many things in life. When driving we must pay attention to what we are doing or else we'll get a ticket, get in a wreck, or even miss our turn. We must pay attention to our gages or we could run out of gas, oil, or even over heat.

Spiritually speaking, we too can get in serious trouble, if we do not pay attention. 1Peter 5:8 gives clear instructions on how to handle a situation and the reason why it is necessary:

"be sober and alert, because the enemy prowls around like a lion seeking someone to eat."

Making one wrong choice in life can be devastating like a domino effect. It could be something small that we don't even think much of at the time but can turn into something huge that can ultimately tear apart our lives and those around us. In 2 Samuel Chapter 11, David makes a bad choice that kept getting worse.

2 Samuel 11:2-5

One evening David got up from his bed and walked around on the roof of the palace. From the roof he saw a woman bathing. The woman was very beautiful, and David sent someone to find out about her. The man said, "She is Bathsheba, the daughter of Eliam and the wife of Uriah(I) the Hittite." Then David sent messengers to get her. She came to him, and he slept with her. (Now she was purifying herself from her monthly uncleanness.) Then she went back home. The woman conceived and sent word to David, saying, "I am pregnant."

Some would say that David was paying too much attention; I say he wasn't paying enough attention to what was right in God's eyes. Chapter 11 reveals that David tried to cover it up by trying to get her husband, Uriah, who was off fighting in the war to come home, hoping that he would come home and sleep with Bathsheba and would think that the child was his. But Uriah refused; he felt his place was with his troops, fighting alongside them. So David ordered Uriah on the front lines, knowing that Uriah more than likely would be killed in battle, and he did. So David took Bathsheba as his wife.

Note the last two verses in Chapter 11:

Vs. 26-27

When Uriah's wife heard that her husband was dead, she mourned for him. After the time of mourning was over, David had her brought to his house, and she became his wife and bore him a son. But the thing David had done displeased the Lord.

David had displeased the Lord! He displeased the Lord because of his own selfish desires, because he paid more attention on him rather than God. He reacted without thinking and was definitely not focused on God. He allowed Satan to work in his life because his life wasn't in the will of God. He wasn't paying attention to his spiritual life.

FOCUS ON HOPE

John 7:25-31

At that point some of the people of Jerusalem began to ask, "Isn't this the man they are trying to kill? 26 Here he is, speaking publicly, and they are not saying a word to him. Have the authorities really concluded that he is the Messiah? 27 But we know where this man is from; when the Messiah comes, no one will know where he is from." 28 Then Jesus, still teaching in the temple courts, cried out, "Yes, you know me, and you know where I am from. I am not here on my own authority, but he who sent me is true. You do not know him, 29 but I know him because I am from him and he sent me." 30 At this they tried to seize him, but no one laid a hand on him, because his hour had not yet come. 31 Still, many in the crowd believed in him. They said, "When the Messiah comes, will he perform more signs than this man?"

There was confusion and beliefs around Jesus. Whether we find confusion or belief depends upon what we focus on. They heard him teach. They heard the rumors and were confused. What He was saying was Messiah-like. Yet, the rulers who sought to kill Him were not accepting. Nobody was stopping Him, or even challenging Him.

Emotions were running high. But feelings are not reliable to take people to Jesus. If you depend upon feelings, in the end, you will be disappointed. They thought they knew Jesus because they knew His earthly history. They knew his mother, father, brothers, and sisters, and they knew His home town, the occupation He was trained in.

Jesus said,

"Oh, you think you know me? You don't really know me because you do not know the Father."

This was very difficult for a Jewish person to accept.

EXPERIENCE IS A GOOD TEACHER, BUT IT IS NOT PERFECT

How many times does God use a new way to do His things? People think they know you. They thought they knew Jesus' background and training. These people even thought they had the background and training to know the truth.

2 Corinthians 5:17

Therefore, if anyone is in Christ, he is a new creation; old things have passed away; behold, all things have become new.

HATRED IS A POWERFUL THING, BUT GOD IS MORE POWERFUL

If you rely on your background and training, it will fall short in the end. The haters anger boiled over. They tried to grab Jesus, but they didn't have the power. They were determined to end this, but God had not determined it yet.

Some people live by determination. There are good and bad descriptions of this. If you are depending upon sheer determination, you will fall short in the end. When some looked at Jesus, they saw a phony, a liar, a deceiver. Some saw Him as a trouble-maker. Because He went against their feelings, experience, background, and training, even their determination to be lords of their own lives.

Jesus was not well accepted, because He represented hope. There was no greater evidence that Jesus was the Messiah than the works He performed, His teachings, His love and compassion, His humility and His strength.

In the end, we stand empty handed, nothing at our resources, with nothing but hope. That can be enough. If you believe in Jesus and call upon Him to save you, hope will pave the way. But hope is more than just wishing.

Romans 5:5

Our hope does not disappoint, because the love of God has been poured out in our hearts by the Holy Spirit who was given to us.

The Hebrews writer said, *"And we desire that each one of you show the same diligence to the full assurance of hope until the end."* That *"Full assurance of hope"* is not the way we use the word "Hope" today. It is an anticipation; not a wish. It is an assurance, confidence, when all appears to contradict.

Peter tells us to be alert because the enemy prowls around us. Satan has us in his targets and is alert and ready to devour us. We need to be alert as well, knowing that Satan is among us, we cannot take our focus off God.

There is an accelerated success waiting for us, and we don't want to be the ones who miss it because our focus was removed from the path of seeing beyond our present wilderness. Our trust and faith in God will shield us from all hurt, harm, and danger.

REFLECTIONS

1. What can you do to leave the wilderness in front of your distracters?

2. Name some positive things that keep you focused beyond the wilderness.

3. What can be done to stop the negative thought patterns from entering your mind?

4. What causes God to become displeased with you?

5. What are some of the results of your spiritual life not receiving enough attention?

6. Your feelings are still a part of your makeup, so why is it not a good idea to rely on them?

11

TRUST AND FAITH

I have learned over the years that when one's mind is made up, this diminishes fear.
—Rosa Parks

In this season of accelerated success there is no more shortage. I have no idea how God is going to do what He said, but I am bold enough to step out in faith and trust Him knowing that He is going to do what He said. That means I do not need to worry about what anyone else is saying. I am depending on God; my trust is in Him.

Trust is earned and learned; it does not happen overnight.

I have learned over the years to trust in the God I serve. My trust did not start overnight. When you start walking with God and seeing how He has been faithful in the past, and He is still keeping His word.

God does not waiver or cast a shadow of doubt, and He has allowed you to overcome many obstacles that you know you did not deserve. It was because of Him that you were able to come through tough times.

You know you can trust God to take care of you. He is responsible for your accelerated success to happen according to His plan and purpose. You must be willing to believe God through your faith in His Word. It may mean not being able to see how God is going to move on your behalf, and you do not know who He is going to use.

Some Christians do not see themselves as the person who God will bless beyond their scope of knowledge. They go through life thinking everything will be accomplished in an inferior or normal way when God has a bigger plan, an accelerated track set to get them to their destiny at a quicker time.

When the Israelites were in bondage for 430 years, God had to remind them about His promise to their forefathers and how He would give them the land. He predestined it for their generation to possess. But it required them to have something called *trust*. They had to take a journey of trust with Moses through the wilderness all those years in order to receive the promise.

Faith Believes.

Judges 6:22 (NLT, Second Edition)
When Gideon realized that it was the angel of the Lord, he cried out, "Oh, Sovereign Lord, I'm doomed! I have seen the angel of the Lord face to face!"

Judges 17:6 (NLT, Second Edition)
In those days Israel had no king; all the people did whatever seemed right in their own eyes.

Faith does not question the angel.

Gideon questioned the angel with doubt in his heart. That was a big mistake because it hindered him from allowing the angel to answer his questions. He waivered in his faith in God and it caused doubt and fear to overtake him.

Judges 6:13 (NLT, Second Edition)

"Sir," Gideon replied, "if the Lord is with us, why has all this happened to us? And where are all the miracles our ancestors told us about? Didn't they say, 'The Lord brought us up out of Egypt'? But now the Lord has abandoned us and handed us over to the Midianites."

Faith does not question God about the "how".

Gideon questioned God when he questioned the angel, who was only God's messenger. The messenger is not as important as the person who sent the message. Questioning and doubting comes from a lack of faith in the messenger.

Isaiah 7:11-12 (NKJV)

"Ask a sign for yourself from the Lord your God; ask it either in the depth or in the height above." But Ahaz said, "I will not ask, nor will I test the Lord!"

Matthew 4:7 (Amplified Bible)

Jesus said to him, On the other hand, it is written also, You shall not tempt, test thoroughly, or try exceedingly the Lord your God.

Acts 15:10 (Amplified Bible)

Now then, why do you try to test God by putting a yoke on the necks of the disciples, such as neither our forefathers nor we [ourselves] were able to endure?

Because God is the tester of our hearts not the other way around, you cannot approach Him and act like you are God. Gideon declared that God left them to their enemies. His thoughts of God were negative. Remember Zechariah the father of John, the Baptist, instead of believing every word of the angel he doubted him and asked how. If it is a miracle, it cannot be answered with logic. He tried logical thinking to accept a miracle, which will not work.

Faith is not living by sight.

Faith will not work if we still use our five senses.

Faith is our sixth sense that is always contrary to the five senses.

Faith does not ask for signs.

Gideon asked for signs.

Judges 6:36-40 (NLT, Second Edition)

Then Gideon said to God, "If you are truly going to use me to rescue Israel as you promised, prove it to me in this way. I will put a wool fleece on the threshing floor tonight. If the fleece is wet with dew in the morning but the ground is dry, then I will know that you are going to help me rescue Israel as you promised."

There were many signs. When Gideon got up early the next morning, he squeezed the fleece and wrung out a whole bowlful of water. Then he said to God,

"Please don't be angry with me, but let me make one more request. Let me use the fleece for one more test. This time let the fleece remain dry while the ground around it is wet with dew."

That night God did as Gideon asked. The fleece was dry in the morning, but the ground was covered with dew.

Signs are for unbelievers.

But for us who are of faith, we no longer need convincing, for we approach God by faith knowing it pleases Him.

Faith does not need to see it to believe.

For Gideon, to see was to believe.

Judges 6:22 (NLT, Second Edition)
When Gideon realized that it was the angel of the Lord, he cried out, "Oh, Sovereign Lord, I'm doomed! I have seen the angel of the Lord face to face!"

Gideon never had faith, not from the beginning.

Faith responds in love not fear.

Instead of responding in love, Gideon responded in fear.

Judges 8:29-31 (NLT, Second Edition)
Then Gideon son of Joash returned home. He had seventy sons born to him, for he had many wives. He also had a concubine in Shechem, who gave birth to a son, whom he named Abimelech.

Gideon did not have perfect love in his heart, which is why it was filled with fear. You should never doubt God if you want to have a good future. Learn to trust God with no questions or signs. If God says you are more than a conqueror, then you are. Believe His Word without requiring a sign or a confirmation. Trust Him and walk by faith so you can make a smooth transition into the success that is waiting for you.

REFLECTIONS

1. Explain how trusting God is a better way of life for you?

2. Why is fear the opposite of faith?

3. What has been your biggest challenge in walking by faith?

4. Have you ever had a Gideon experience? If so, how did it affect your faith?

5. God can show us a sign, but what are the benefits of trusting in Him and His word?

PART IV

KEYS TO ADVANCING THE KINGDOM

12

TRANSITIONING

*In order to succeed, your desire for success should be
greater than your fear of failure.*
—Bill Cosby

How many times have we seen someone try to make a
change, but after they started they became discouraged
and gave up? It happens to all of us. Throughout our
lives we want to make many changes even if they are difficult to make. When we fail to make a change we want, it
may not be because we "didn't want it badly enough."
Maybe we failed to make a change because we got
caught up in unexpected emotions that come with transitions. Maybe we gave up because we couldn't change
the stories we tell ourselves about who we really are.

TRANSITION STAGES

a) Endings
b) Neutral Zones
c) New Beginnings

Transitions do not start as long as we are stuck in denial or fantasy. "Endings" force us to let go of the old way. Beyond letting go, we have to get through an uncomfortable in-between time called the "Neutral Zones," when the old way is gone but the new way doesn't yet wholly work or feel comfortable. This phase is where a new way of doing things, a new identity, or a new opportunity for growth and progress comes into focus.

The "New Beginnings" phase initially brings a feeling of finally having "arrived," mixed with anxiety about backsliding. New values, attitudes, and most of all, new identities have emerged. The "New Beginning" does not erase the past; a new identity has emerged that includes a new and different understanding of what the past means.

A REALITY CHECK

Transitioning from the wilderness stage for Joshua is where God's promise becomes a reality. Seeing God's covenant people posses the land, we can learn how the promise became a reality to them and apply much of the same ways to our lives too.

Standing at the Red Sea was going to end 430 years of slavery. Standing on the banks of the Jordan River was where forty years of wilderness existence was ending. It was the end of forty years of many things such as follows:

a) Walking in a circle going nowhere fast.

b) Striving and never arriving.

c) Walking by sight.

d) Independent living.

e) Never being assured of victory over the enemy.

f) Being constantly reminded of past failures.

g) Fear.

h) Self centered existence where life was all about them.

Although it was the end for most of them, it was not for the tribe of Gad and the one-half tribe of Manasseh. They would never occupy the land. The Promise of God would be only words and never substance for them. These people opted out of God's plan and Him carrying out His purpose through them. They chose to opt for something much less than having fullness of joy, peace, a meaningful relationship, and enjoying the milk and honey of being in fellowship with Him.

Many people in covenant with God have settled for less than His best for them. But for those who were going to cross Jordan, the end of the wilderness was just three days away. Imagine in three days they would be going on the greatest adventure of their lives. The problem was that they did not know what was ahead of them.

I do not know whether the Israelites would have believed the things that were going to happen even if God had been specific. He had already promised to be with them, but it was as if they did not know the great work God was going to do on their behalf to ensure that they would posses this Promised Land. In their minds, they only saw walls of fortified cities fall before their eyes. Mercy and grace was in a defeat, because they could not see their enemies being terrified of them so they could begin to enter God's rest. The issue is in knowing what was going on with the Israelites in this transition time, before they crossed over from wilderness living to Canaan living.

FREEDOM AND FEAR

Transition time can be a bittersweet experience because freedom and fear can happen at the same time. We go from trusting our own resources and ourselves to meet our daily needs to trusting God for life. We go from our own do-it-yourself projects to being able to trust God to do them for us and through us.

Perhaps this is your transition time, going from religion to relationship, from trying to trusting, from self-reliance to God reliance. Letting go may be challenging, but letting God is sure to be most rewarding since His Word is sure. He cannot lie and He backs up His Word.

FOUR KEYS TO TRANSITIONING

Let us examine four key things that the Children of Israel had to do during their time of transition.

1. FACE THE JORDAN

a. It was un-crossable just like the Red Sea.

This was the flood stage; no resources; they had to wait there for three days and look at this uncrossable river. Have you ever had one of those in your life? Could it be a thing, an incident, or a person whom you have not been able to forgive; you just cannot get around or over the incident? Maybe it was something that happened a long time ago when you were younger, or it might have been recently, but you have not been able to move ahead because of this un-crossable river.

b. It stood between them and freedom from the wilderness.

It was the last physical barrier to cross before the promise becomes a reality. What do they do now? What are their options when they sit there? Not one thing THEY can do to get across in and of themselves.

2. EITHER TRUST GOD OR GO BACK AND STAY IN THE WILDERNESS

The un-crossable is something that we cannot handle; things such as the unresolved anger, the hurt that happened many years ago, the mistake that you wish you had never made, and all the other things that you still regret.

God can fix and make changes beyond our reach.

We cannot change our fixes, but God can fix and make changes. Face the Jordan, not with despair, but with hope for deliverance from all evil that has come against you and tried to distract you from entering your new season.

3. FOCUS ON GOD

a. He would be their solution to crossing over the Jordan.

Isaiah 26:3
You will keep in perfect peace those whose minds are steadfast, because they trust in you.

b. How do I focus on God?

We must focus on His Word, prayer, and making a choice. That is what the early covenant people did. When Nehemiah was faced with the wall he called on the Lord. We must remove our focus from how we feel to become totally focused on God.

4. FACE YOUR OWN SELF

a. Consecrate yourselves; set yourselves apart.

Why? For tomorrow you will see great wonders among you; set yourselves apart from the mindset of the wilderness. It was time for them to leave walking by sight to begin to walk by faith trusting God not only as their Savior but also as life.

b. They needed to know.

God was going to cut the water off when the Priests rested their feet in the water. Nothing was going to happen until they were willing to rest their feet in the water; it is called faith.

Standing at the Jordan was a defining moment in the lives of God's people. It was a moment when they faced the reality of where they were, and they had to decide whether they move forward or go back to the wilderness.

What is your defining moment in this season of receiving God's promise? No matter what your circumstances may look like today, you must believe that God wants you to walk in a newness of life beyond the wilderness stage and into His promise of acceleration.

God didn't take the children of Israel the shortest route to the Promised Land because He knew they were not prepared for war. God could see the big picture. He knew if He took them the shortest way, their enemies would be too powerful, and they would be defeated. So on purpose, God took them a longer route to protect and strengthen them so that they could fulfill their destiny

If something is not happening on your timetable, understand that God knows what He is doing. He has your best interest at heart. While in transition, stop trying to figure everything out. Instead, turn it over to God. Say like David:

Psalm 31:15
My times are in your hands; deliver me from the hands of my enemies, from those who pursue me.

Believe that at the appointed time, you will see God's Promise fulfilled in your life. Ask God to help you guard your heart as you bring your concerns, anxieties, and questions to Him, and ask for wisdom. Submit yourself to God and resist the devil, so that he will flee from you (James 5:7). Resist the spirit of fear and intimidation that shows itself as anxiety and wrong thoughts during this transitioning phase.

REFLECTIONS

1. Have you ever experienced an un-crossable river in your life? If so, how did you deal with it?

2. Why is it not a good idea to combine self-reliance tactics and trusting God in reaching your accelerated success?

3. God's Word admonishes us to consecrate ourselves. Why is this important in your walk with God?

4. How do you keep your mind renewed?

5. Are you challenged in the area of being focused on God? If so, how do you deal with it?

13

WISDOM

Knowledge can be communicated, but not wisdom. One can find it, live it, be fortified by it, do wonders through it, but one cannot communicate and teach it.
—Hermann Hesse

This is a season of success for many saints in numerous ways. Some will transition into a place of greater influence, and there are many whose times of private fellowship with God have prepared them for their public advancement.

Psalm 75 says our promotion comes from God for His Kingdom purposes to be fulfilled in our lives. Therefore, we are promoted for one reason, which is to advance

God's agenda. It cannot be for the purpose of accomplishing our own agenda or anyone else's. Our goal should be to have God's divine purpose fulfilled in our lives.

Psalm 75:6-7
No one from the east or the west or from the desert can exalt themselves. 7 It is God who judges: He brings one down, he exalts another.

There are times when a promotion seems like it is a demotion. Each time Joseph went to the pit, and then to prison, he was always a step closer to his destiny. The Apostle Paul's promotion sent him to imprisonment and later positioned him to be on death row in Rome. He would, however, eventually have the Emperor of the known world captivated as an audience before his death.

Promotion does not always glitter, and is rarely glamorous. It is guaranteed to bring us to a new level of warfare both internally and externally. That is why we cannot advance without wisdom from God. This principle is illustrated below:

Proverbs 4:7-8

The beginning of wisdom is this: Get wisdom. Though it cost all you have, get understanding. 8 Cherish her, and she will exalt you; embrace her, and she will honor you.

What exactly is "wisdom"? Webster's dictionary defines "wisdom" as the ability to discern what is true or right. Godly wisdom is learning to see things as God sees them. It is called the "Big Picture" mentality. When we have a hearing ear we can ask the question, "What's really happening here?" and have the faith to hear and communicate the answer.

Wisdom is what we need to fulfill God's purpose for our life. God has a design for each of us. We need wisdom to fulfill that design.

HOW DOES ONE ACQUIRE WISDOM?

The place to begin is the fear of the Lord. Wisdom begins with the fear of the Lord.

Proverbs 1:7

The fear of the Lord is the beginning of knowledge, but fools despise wisdom and discipline.

In this verse, the words, "knowledge," "wisdom," and "discipline" are all being used as synonyms, to describe the same thing. Most Bible teachers view this verse as the motto or theme of the entire book of Proverbs. Every wise saying we find in Proverbs goes back to this foundational principle.

The fear of the Lord has two sides: One side is to hate evil, to hate sin, and to avoid sin at all cost. Another side is to delight in doing God's will.

Psalm 112:2

Blessed is the man who fears the LORD, who finds great delight in his commands.

To fear God means to view God with deep and healthy respect as shown in one's hatred of evil, and love for what God wants. Another requirement for receiving wisdom is found in Proverbs 4:7-8. We are commanded to "get wisdom," "get understanding," "esteem wisdom," and "embrace wisdom."

Proverbs 4:7-8

The beginning of wisdom is this: Get wisdom. Though it cost all you have, get understanding. 8 Cherish her, and she will exalt you; embrace her, and she will honor you.

The pursuit of wisdom is one of the most important things in life that we can do. It is more important than making a lot of money. If we honor wisdom, like a king, wisdom will lift us up. We pursue wisdom by boldly asking God for it.

In the New Testament from the Bible we learn that if we lack in wisdom, we should ask God for it, and he'll give it to us if we ask him in faith (James 1:5). So we start our pursuit by admitting that we lack wisdom and asking God for it. Often we lack wisdom because we're not humble enough to ask God for it.

We can also pursue wisdom by reading the Bible. Another way we pursue wisdom is by observation. Most of the wise sayings in the book of Proverbs did not come by direct revelation from God. He didn't reveal these wise sayings through dreams or visions or an audible voice. Instead, He revealed them through people's observational skills, what you might call sanctified common sense.

Most often Proverbs worked this way. A person is walking along the road and he notices the yard of a lazy person. He notices that the yard is overgrown with weeds, and the walls around the yard are broken down and in need of repair. Then the observer tells us:

Prov. 24:30-34
I saw and I considered it, I looked and I received instruction: a little sleep, a little slumber, and poverty will come upon you like a robber.

That's how most of the Proverbs came, from careful observation combined with reflection. So observe the world around you, watch how people respond, what kind of consequences come from certain actions.

A final way we can pursue wisdom is by reading. Many of the wise sayings came during Solomon's reign, when Israel became an international superpower and Israel's leaders encountered the wise sayings of the Egyptians and other nations. They accepted those wise sayings that they felt were consistent with fear of Yahweh, and eventually these wise sayings were incorporated into our own Bibles.

WORLDLY WISDOM

There is a worldly wisdom and it is not always truthful or wise. For example, the world says, "Eat, drink and be merry for you only go 'around' once in life." In other words, live it up, do whatever you want because some day you'll die and life will be over. If we were to follow those instructions, we would be going against the plan and purposes that God has established for our lives to be fulfilled.

James 4:13-17

Now listen, you who say, "Today or tomorrow we will go to this or that city, spend a year there, carry on business and make money. Why, you do not even know what will happen tomorrow. What is your life? You are a mist that appears for a little while and then vanishes. Instead, you ought to say, "If it is the Lord's will, we will live and do this or that." As it is, you boast and brag. All such boasting is evil. Anyone, then, who knows the good he ought to do and doesn't do it, sins.

James is giving us the wisdom of our eternal God. He is saying, *"Life is short. Include God in everything you do. Seek God's will for your life."*

God is our Creator. We begin life with Him and end life with Him, and we need to sandwich Him into our lives every day. Rightfully, we should focus on Him continually, as in *"pray without ceasing"* (I Thess. 5:17, KJV).

The greatest wisdom of all, of course, is from God. The wisdom of this world says many things, which some people believe, but we need the wisdom of God to avoid evil in this world and not be led astray from our faith in Christ.

We must listen for wisdom wherever it speaks and gain from it. God's wisdom is infinite and we have a right to ask for it. We need His divine wisdom to guide us in knowing how to release the weights of this world from our shoulders so we can soar like eagles and reach our goal of accelerated success.

REFLECTIONS

1. What is God's purpose for your success?

2. How can you advance the Kingdom of God with wisdom?

3. Is to fear God a good thing?

4. How can you pursue wisdom from God?

5. What method can be used to determine the difference between the wisdom of God and worldly wisdom?

14

WEIGHTS

When everything seems to be going against you, remember that the airplane takes off against the wind, not with it.
—Henry Ford

Weights are not necessarily sins but they are a hindrance that can slow you down. They slow your progress in reaching your next destination. When you find your journey is taking too long because of the weights, it can cause you to get discouraged especially when we carry weights that we do not need. They may be the things that get us off track.

Hebrews 12:1-2

Therefore, since we are surrounded by such a great cloud of witnesses, let us throw off everything that hinders and the sin that so easily entangles. And let us run with perseverance the race marked out for us, 2 fixing our eyes on Jesus, the pioneer and perfecter of faith. For the joy set before him he endured the cross, scorning its shame, and sat down at the right hand of the throne of God.

The writer of the book of Hebrews calls his hearers to *"throw off everything that hinders and the sin that so easily entangles."* In line with the sports imagery of verse 1, the word could refer to a runner stripping off burdensome clothing or losing excess bodily fat. A person had to get rid of anything that would "hinder breathing or the free movement of the limbs."

We must lay aside "everything that hinders" if the faith race is to be run triumphantly. And we should get rid of the *"entangling sin."* No specific sin is mentioned because any sin hinders the development of our faith.

Sometimes things weigh us down that we should find easy to let go. Instead, we tend to hold on to them with dear life not realizing how much it is hindering us from moving forward.

THE WEIGHT OF UNFORGIVENESS

Some people allow thoughts to become a weight. Forgiveness is a common weight. Some people allow themselves to become very upset and hurt when mistreated by others, and they find it difficult to forgive. Often the spirit of pride causes them to lose their focus on the things they are called to do.

Mark 11:25
And when you stand praying, if you hold anything against anyone, forgive them, so that your Father in heaven may forgive you your sins.

Christians are to be forgiving of others when we are wronged. How do we expect to be forgiven ourselves of the sin within our lives if we can't forgive others?

When we don't forgive, our weights become even heavier because of the sins we carry around and they all begin to add up. A small white lie here, an adulterous thought there, a slip of the tongue, and we pack it all in and hold on to it because we can't simply forgive others.

People like to pick up the weight of unforgiveness and carry it throughout their lives, and when their pride is hurt, they will gladly add unforgiveness to their load and tell themselves that they will never forgive so and so for as long as they live. Sometimes they pretend that the weight isn't heavy and they go on about their happy lives carrying un-forgiveness. They think by holding onto certain things that it will make them feel better about how they were treated.

Nothing is further from the truth except that carrying extra weight will sooner or later get the best of them.

Likewise, isn't this what we do as well when we place the heaviness of unforgiveness into our lives? We feel that we can't survive without it and we pack it deep down inside and we go through life carting the heaviness around thinking the whole time that we are okay. But the truth is we are not okay, we are only hurting ourselves, others, and our relationship with God when we do not simply let go of the unforgiveness in our hearts.

THE WEIGHT OF UNCONFESSED SINS

Unconfessed sin in our lives is like a small pebble in our shoe or a small splinter in our finger. Neither one is big enough to stop us, but they sure can slow us down. Have you ever tried to keep walking or running with a small pebble in your shoe? You can do it, but it hurts and it steals our concentration on what is important.

Unconfessed sins in our life do the same thing. They may not keep us from going to heaven, but they sure know how to make getting there much more difficult.

Unconfessed sin is a robber of joy, a robber of peace, a robber of victory. It keeps us in shame and defeat. It adds weight on our backs that is unnecessary. But there is a cure for the weight of unconfessed sin.

I John 1:9
If we confess our sins, he is faithful and just and will forgive us our sins and purify us from all unrighteousness.

I am not talking about sins that you committed and cannot remember, that would require carrying around a notebook each day if this is what God meant by unconfessed sin. Unconfessed sin is sin that we are aware of and hold onto, not willing to let it go. We hide those sins from others and justify our actions.

UNSPOKEN PRAYERS

We read in Scripture, that we *do not have because we do not ask.* We struggle with finances, our children and family members, our job, our neighbors; the troubles of society and the political issues all around us. We carry them as weights.

Some people have a feeling of unworthiness that keeps their prayers from being offered to God. They may be afraid God would give them what they pray for and they might not be willing to make the changes necessary.

Philippians 4:6
Do not be anxious about anything, but in everything, by prayer and petition, with thanksgiving, present your requests to God.

What prayer do you need to offer to God today to lighten your load? Do not allow your prayers to build up while you clutter your life with negativity. Negativity will only slow you down causing you to feel the burden of a heavy heart.

Matthew 11: 28-30

Come to me, all you who are weary and burdened, and I will give you rest. 29 Take my yoke upon you and learn from me, for I am gentle and humble in heart, and you will find rest for your souls. 30 For my yoke is easy and my burden is light.

1 Peter 5: 6-7

Humble yourselves, therefore, under God's mighty hand, that he may lift you up in due time. 7 Cast all your anxiety on him because he cares for you.

All unforgiveness, unconfessed sin, and unspoken prayers will only weigh you down. I pray that you will choose to simply unload the weights by giving them to Jesus. If you don't allow Him to help, you will live a heavy miserable, life. You will find no rest for your soul. But, Jesus has already done what it takes to receive rest for your soul. He died a horrible death, taking the sin and guilt of everyone, destroying them once and for all. You can have your sin and the guilt taken away this day. You can let Jesus carry it to the cross for you. Here is what you must do:

✳ **Believe that Jesus is God's Son.**

✳ **Decide to change your ways, follow God's path instead of your own.**

✳ **Remove the unnecessary weights and hand them over to Jesus.**

God wants you to have faith in Him, that He is the one we run to; He is the one who can take all the excess weight off our shoulders and keep us advancing toward the Promise.

REFLECTIONS

1. Describe some hindrances to your faith.

2. Are you carrying weights? Do they draw attention or sympathy from others?

3. How does an unforgiving spirit affect you?

4. How do you deal with un-confessed sins? Have you ever used them to accelerate your success?

5. Why do weights generate a heavy heart?

15

ADVANCING TOWARD THE PROMISE

A good archer is known not by his arrows but by his aim.
—Thomas Fuller

Advancing toward the Promise requires being able to run the race that God has set before us. Hebrews Chapter 12 tells us how to run the race to achieve the promise of accelerated success.

Hebrews 12:2
Fixing our eyes on Jesus, the pioneer and perfecter of faith. For the joy set before him he endured the cross, scorning its shame, and sat down at the right hand of the throne of God.

1. RUN WITH ENDURANCE

In the context of the "race," Jesus is the one who has run the path before us and He offers the example of how the race is to be run. He is also the *"author and perfecter of our faith."* This sets Jesus apart from all the examples in Hebrews Chapter 11. This lets us know that He is an initiator, and as the perfecter of faith, Jesus brings it to its intended goal. For this reason, we must keep looking to Him and not the world.

Ultimately, Jesus accomplished the perfection of our faith by his sacrificial death on the cross. He has cleared the path of faith so that we may run it. The way is open, and although hurdles exist, the roadblocks have been removed.

Jesus not only perfected faith but also provided the example of endurance because he looked beyond immediate, painful circumstances to the reward that was ahead. It was the joy that was set before Him that gave Him power to endure the cross.

2. FIX YOUR EYES ON JESUS

Verse 2 explains Jesus as being our example because it says he is the author and finisher of our faith. His life shows us how to fix our eyes on Him when distractions come our way. Jesus did something that is the key to you walking in your next level of success.

The enemy allows you to be distracted to get you off track and lose your joy. So he will do all kinds of things to slow your life down and have you making decisions that are off course with where you are going. The decisions you make today can have consequences that may not impact you until two or three years later. You could feel good about the decision because of where things are until the consequences hit you later in life.

Though you may repent immediately after discovering things are not on course, the change sometimes is not as quick. It may be a slow process and you aren't ready for that slow turn. You've changed over those few years and have taken on different habits, different disciplines, you think differently, you've got different friends, different relationships. Now you have to consider a variety of things such as: If you go down the first road you're going to have a certain group of friends. If you go down another road you're going to have a certain group of friends, then God tells you that the road you have been on is the wrong road and you have been on it for three years.

All the people who you have accumulated on that course are now really no good for where God is telling you to go. It is time to break off relationships; you have to separate yourself from some people. That becomes another process before you can turn in a new direction. Some people reach that place in life and they want God to just do it for them. That is not how God works, and what we want to look at is how we receive what God promised. It was the joy that was set before Jesus that allowed Him to endure the cross despised and ashamed.

If you do not follow Jesus, you will become discouraged and slow down. Sometimes doubt enters and it's against God. You may say, "I know what the Lord said, but when is He going to move. It seems like He's taking forever." Then you start having a conversation with yourself or other people when in the beginning you were having it with the devil. After awhile his voice starts sounding like your own. So you think you are hearing yourself talking about your situation when it is really Satan.

This process takes place when a person gets off course. It did not happen in one day, it takes time because you're negotiating mentally and emotionally about the decision that you are making. No longer do you see what is set before you. It sometimes helps if you have a picture of what is before you, it helps you to keep moving. When the picture is removed you might become discouraged because you cannot see everything. So get a picture.

3. OVERCOME INIQUITIES

What is iniquity?

Some people think that sin is the same as iniquity. Isaiah describes the effect of each.

Isaiah 59:2
"... but your iniquities have separated you from God; your sins have hidden his face from you so that he will not hear."

Jeremiah says iniquities have kept good things from us. So getting rid of iniquities will take us to the next level of success.

Jeremiah 5:25
Your wrongdoings have kept these away; your sins have deprived you of good.

Ezekiel 36:33-37

Thus says the Lord God: On the day that I cleanse you from all your iniquities, I will cause the cities to be inhabited, and the waste places shall be rebuilt. 34 And the land that was desolate shall be tilled, instead of being the desolation that it was in the sight of all who passed by. 35 And they will say, "This land that was desolate has become like the garden of Eden, and the waste and desolate and ruined cities are now fortified and inhabited." 36 Then the nations that are left all around you shall know that I am the Lord; I have rebuilt the ruined places and replanted that which was desolate. I am the Lord; I have spoken, and I will do it. 37 "Thus says the Lord God: This also I will let the house of Israel ask me to do for them: to increase their people like a flock."

When the land enjoys the benefits of the people's cleansing, the impact on the land is not simply on its fertility but the cityscape is renewed as well as the landscape. The fertility of the land will be restored.

Notice how verse 37 also talks about numeric increase (like a flock). It all starts with a very simple thing, God says, *"Thus says the Lord God: On the day that I cleanse you from all your iniquities..."*

This seems to be too simple to be true. So if we are cleansed from iniquities the blessing will come.

Exodus 34:7

Keeping mercy for thousands, forgiving iniquity and transgression and sin, and that will by no means clear the guilty; visiting the iniquity of the fathers upon the children, and upon the children's children, unto the third and to the fourth generation.

❋ Iniquity—Perversion

Gross immorality or injustice; wickedness.

The Hebrew meaning is perverseness, bowed down, twisted; to be bent or crooked; to be wrung out of course. The word "iniquity" ('avon in Hebrew) is used to express how a human heart is not holy—not set apart, not perfect, not godly.

❋ Transgression—Rebellion

A violation of a law, command, or duty: The exceeding of due bounds or limits.

The Hebrew meaning of transgression is a willful deviation from, and therefore rebellion against, the path of godly living. The Greek meaning of transgression is: *To go beyond; Overstepping the limits.* This word very strongly links with rebellion and disobedience.

Transgressions are more potent than just sinning and are the next step into further permanent bondage. Transgressions are related to trespass, which is a willful violation of the law (human or Godly law).

❋ Sin = Missing the mark

Insufficient to satisfy a requirement or meet a need resulting from such inadequacy.

The English word for sin is derived from *archery*. The archer would draw the bow and shoot the arrow toward the target. If he missed the mark, then the overseeing official would yell "sin." The Hebrew meaning of sin is slipping away from where you should be.

Prov. 25:28
Whoever has no rule over his spirit is like a city, broken down, without walls.

Sin refers to an action, something that happens in the real world. Iniquity is an attitude of the heart. Iniquity will eventually lead us to sin. Iniquity is the same as unholiness. Any area of our life that is not set apart for God is an area of iniquity.

Scripture talks about Sin (singular) and Iniquities (plural). Jesus came to take away our sin but the iniquities of our heart are removed through a process of cleansing that we Christians call "Holiness" or living "Holy lives."

❋ **Forgiveness of sin is instantaneous but cleansing of iniquities is progressive and takes time.**

❋ **How to get rid of iniquities.**

God accepts you just as you are, He loves you even if you have iniquities but He cannot bless you if you keep having wrong attitudes that burst from your heart.

James 1:23-25

For if anyone is a hearer of the word and not a doer, he is like a man who looks intently at his natural face in a mirror. 24 For he looks at himself and goes away and at once forgets what he was like. 25 But the one who looks into the perfect law, the law of liberty, and perseveres, being no hearer who forgets but a doer who acts, he will be blessed in his doing.

If you want to get rid of your iniquities you need to be washed by the Word. God places Pastors, Evangelists, Teachers, Apostles, and Prophets in your way so you can identify the iniquities of your heart and act upon it. God wants to bless you by removing the iniquities out of your life.

4. PREPARE TO WALK ALONE

I believe that everybody who has been born into the world came here for a purpose. There are those who find that purpose but are afraid to walk into it.

What is it that causes people to be so fearful of walking into the one thing that they were placed in this world to do? It is the fear of walking alone. They have never been this way before and do not know what to expect so they resolve to stay with what they know best. It is important that God is leading you in the direction that you desire to go.

Ps 37:23
The Lord makes firm the steps of the one who delights in him;

Each journey that you take in life involves walking into it. Every adventure is a step into what you haven't done before and it calls for overcoming the fear of walking alone. You can be certain that there is no need to fear if God is ordering your steps. Your faith must be strong to overcome fear.

Isaiah 40:29

He gives strength to the weary and increases the power of the weak.

There are some places in your life that you're going to have to walk alone. Although many people may be around you, there is still the feeling that without God you are alone. You cannot depend on your own ability or you will definitely fail. You must be empowered by God if you are going to be successful at what you set out to do.

Whatever success you set out to achieve, if God is leading you, you don't have to worry about being alone. He will go with you and surely help you to overcome the fear of walking alone. Stay on course applying His wisdom in every aspect of your journey, and watch for the signs of the times for He is faithful to see you reach the finish line.

REFLECTIONS

1. How do you train for your endurance race?

2. When you become unfocused, how can you get back on track?

3. What are the results of removing iniquity from your life?

16

SIGNS

The question isn't who is going to let me;
it's who is going to stop me.
—Ayn Rand

Here you are advancing toward the Promise. If you
are wondering how close you are to your promotion, just
take note of the following signs:

Giants always show up
when it's time to be promoted.

Before your promotion there is something you've got
to deal with. David was faced with a giant at the time of

his promotion. Giants always show up when it's time for you to be promoted.

We all know this story of David and Goliath in 1 Samuel Chapter 17, how God used a brave young man full of faith to fight a giant for God and His people, Israel. David is not the only person to come up against a giant. All believers will find themselves face to face with big challenges, and quite often. But on a few rare occasions you find yourself staring into the eyes of a Goliath!

The Philistines had invaded the Israelites' territory. Goliath stood and defied the army of God, and they are huddled together, frightened, and did not attempt to do anything to eliminate him. Goliath stood waving his spear high in the air challenging someone to defend the name of God.

The enemy is all around us today. We are faced with Goliaths from every angle. We have been given weapons that will kill any giant that stands before us; thus, we must use what God has given us.

Verse 40 of 1 Samuel Chapter 17 tells us how David reached down into the brook, picked up five smooth stones and then proceeded to kill the giant. Our thoughts seem to be more on the fact that Goliath is out there, rather than how to defeat that giant. Here are some strategies:

- We must be filled with the Spirit of God and trust God to get the job done.

- We must do small jobs as though they were big jobs and when the big job comes, God will let us do them as though they were small.

- Attempt great things for God, and expect great things FROM God! David was a sheep herder, but he became a giant killer.

PAST EXPERIENCE

(1 Samuel Chapter 17: 32-37)

David had proven the power of god in his past life. He knew the victory could be won. David was not fearful of the armor or Goliath's giant size. He had faced giant-sized enemies many times before meeting Goliath. David had received Divine strength before and had proven it was sufficient.

THE WORD OF GOD
(Vs. 45-47)
It was on a hillside while caring for the sheep that David was alone with God. He played his harp while worshipping God.

A BIG VISION
(Vs. 47-48; 51 & 54)
We must not be satisfied with what God has done in the past. We must continue on attempting big things for God.

Psalm 81:10
I am the Lord your God, who brought you up out of Egypt. Open wide your mouth and I will fill it.

PROBLEM SOLVER
You are on the verge of being successful, but you haven't solved the problem that will make you succeed. You see it but you haven't yet dealt with it. People want to be successful in the wilderness, but they need to come out of it in order to be successful.

David went through the process of being fitted to wear Saul's armor. Some people want to wear someone else's armor when they simply need to just be themselves. God's going to use them; they do not need to be like someone else.

Promotion comes in the middle of a battle.

In the moment of promotion, David was avoiding being hit by javelins, and at first he laughed. The giant also laughed and asked whether he was a dog that they sent a boy out to do a man's job. David did not have a sword in his hand, not even a helmet to protect his head. In the natural, the giant had a sword and a spear but David came in the name of the Lord.

Proverbs 18:10
The name of the Lord is a fortified tower; the righteous run to it and are safe.

David was ready for his moment of promotion. When the time came he was in place. He took Goliath's head off. No one expected him to even be able to pick up the sword with one hand.

Those who were watching became angry because David did what he said; they did not know how easy it was. If they had faith in God, they could have been used too. But they feared because of what they saw with their **natural eyes.**

Keep your eyes on the prize.

Do not fear your circumstances by what you fear with your eyes; keep your eyes on the prize. David did not see a giant too big, other than too big to miss.

If you are in a place of being successful and you are being tested, do not run from it. If God chose you, then you are well able to receive the success. When I enter the ring with somebody to fight, I tell them they better be able to put everything they've got on the line, because I am coming with everything. I am going to give all I've got with no holding back.

We are getting ready to touch this nation and the nations of the world. It is up to you to believe it. If you are in the right place at the right time you will too. Do not miss your season of accelerated success.

The Bible says the promises of God are received by faith. Call those things that are not as though they were. Continue to say what God says about you.

Stay in the fight.

I know you have been faced with dilemmas and challenges in your lifetime. I know that it gets tough, I know the road gets rough, and it gets challenging, I know you are faced with things, and you are holding on for dear life. Do not quit; stay in the fight.

Keep the vision in front of you.

Keeping the vision in front of you gives you power to endure so that you can approach your day. You are in a place of promotion. Stay there because God is going to choose you if you choose to believe Him and obey His word.

See the opportunity.

David came to the army's camp and saw that opportunity. That was his choice to go from one level to the next, he made a choice. Every time after that when people thought that he did not know what was going on, he walked around with Goliath's head for a while. He was reminding people of what he was capable of doing. It was also a reminder to him that God gave him the Philistine's head.

You hold the key to your success; walk in it. This is your season, no more shortage; your success has been accelerated. Give God the glory now while you are waiting to see the manifestation of your Kingdom advancement.

REFLECTIONS

1. What signs can you expect to receive when you are about to be promoted?

2. Have you ever lost a fight since you accepted Jesus? If so, how did you handle your defeat?

3. How are your giants defeated now?

4. How can you remain focused when your promotion is right in front of you?

5. You have received your promotion, now what should you do to keep it?

CONCLUSION

We have entered a new season where there is no more shortage because God is accelerating our success causing us to advance in the kingdom of God. Our advancement has nothing to do with going fast but changing how fast we are moving toward our divine promotion in this season.

There has been a shifting in the Spirit realm that is causing God's grace and favor to move on our life just as it did with the Israelites and their deliverance out of the bondage when God moved quickly on their behalf. In one night they got the freedom they needed after hundreds of years in slavery, and they left with jewelry and precious items that could not have been gained on their own accord.

This season of ACCELERATED SUCCESS is where God is bringing His faithful ones to a place of domination that they could not achieve in their own strength. So we must not look on our past but look up toward who holds our future. He is expanding our territory, and we are moving into a good and spacious place where He will be glorified as the only true God.

This is our season; this is our time to expect incredible things. Expect to be promoted far beyond what your eyes can see now or your ears can hear, for you cannot begin to comprehend the quickness of God's manifested power in your life. So get ready for your accelerated success, and embrace this prophetic season in your life.

APPENDIX

SCRIPTURES

CHAPTER 1
Heb. 11:1 NASB; 12:2, 13:8; Luke 6:38; Hosea 4:6

CHAPTER 2
Matt. 12:34; Ps.19:14; Prov. 18:21; Mk. 11:23; Gen. 3:4b; Heb. 4:2; Rom. 10:17

CHAPTER 3
Heb. 4:1-2; Matt. 25:14-30; Hab. 2:4b; Jn. 6:9-11

CHAPTER 4
Book of Exodus; Gn. 6-9

CHAPTER 5
Matt. 7:7-11 NASB; Phil. 2:13 NASB; 2 Pet. 1:5, 8, 12, 15

CHAPTER 6
Num. 13:28-33

CHAPTER 7
I Sam. 16:13; Ch. 17-18; Matt. 6:11; I Pet. 4:12

CHAPTER 8
Heb. 12:1-3; I Cor. 15:58; Heb. 10:23; James 1:6; 2 Tim. 2:16-18; Titus 2:14; 3:8,14; Heb. 13:21; Col. 2:7; I Thess. 4:1; 2 Thess. 1:3; Gal. 4:18; Col. 4:12; I Pet. 3:15; Matt. 25:21; I Jn. 3:1-3; 2 Pet. 3:11-14; Heb. 12:14; Matt. 5:8; I Jn. 3:3; I Pet. 1:16; I Jn. 3:5; Heb. 4:15; 2 Cor. 5:21; I Pet. 2:22; 2 Cor. 7:1; Gal. 5:19-21; Heb. 12:1-3; I Pet. 4:1; 2 Tim. 3:12; I Pet. 4:13; Luke 6:22-23

CHAPTER 9
Jn. 13:15; Rom. 5:6-8; Luke 14:33; Jn. 21:19; Matt. 16:24; Heb. 12:2-4; I Pet. 2:21-23; Jn. 15:12-13; Luke 22:42-44

CHAPTER 10
I Pet. 5:8; 2 Sam. Ch. 11; Jn. 7:25-31; 2 Cor. 5:17; Rom. 5:5

CHAPTER 11
Jud. NLT 2nd Ed: 6:22; 17:6; 6:13; 6:36-40; 6:22: 8:29-31; Isa. 7:11-12 NKJV; Matt. 4:7 AMP; Acts 15:10 AMP;

CHAPTER 12
Isa. 26:3; Ps. 31:15; James 5:7

CHAPTER 13
Ps. 75:6-7; Prov. 4:7-8; Prov. 1:7; Ps. 112:2; Prov. 4:7-8; 24:30-34; James 4:13-17; I Thess. 5:17 KJV

CHAPTER 14
Heb. 12:1-2; Mk. 11:25; I Jn. 1:9; Phil. 4:6; Matt. 11:25; 28-30; I Pet. 5:6-7

CHAPTER 15
Heb. 12:2; Isa. 59:2; Jer. 5:25; Ezek. 36:33-37; Exod. 34:7; Prov. 25:28; James 1:23-25; Ps. 37:23; Isa. 40:29

CHAPTER 16
I Sam. Ch. 17; Ps. 81:10; Prov. 18:10

ABOUT THE AUTHOR

Bishop Stanley M. Williams is Founder and Senior Pastor of The Church 3:20 in Jacksonville, Florida. He and his wife, Dr. E. Denise, shepherd a growing flock of people of all ages, races, and nationalities, and have inspired a unity of saints from varying socioeconomic and political backgrounds.

He earned his Bachelor of Theology from Cornerstone University and Seminary. Moreover, he was ordained in 1986 by Bishop Jeffery Banks, founder of Revival Temple Center of Deliverance in Newark, NJ.

Over the past 25 years of ministry, Bishop Williams has resided on several Boards of organizing churches and Pastoral Fellowship. Bishop Williams is the President of

West Jacksonville Restoration Center, a Non-Profit Organization that reaches out to the nearby communities.

He has traveled throughout the United States teaching in the area of financial and spiritual growth to the many congregations he has come to know. He desires to see people reach their highest potential in the Body of Christ.

Bishop Williams has allowed God to use him for His will and purpose. As a result, he has developed an Evangelistic ministry of anointing and power that has reached the entire United States and Europe. His ministry of healing, deliverance, and restoration has blessed many. Souls have been saved, bodies healed, yokes broken, captives set free, and oppressed delivered under the mighty anointing of this man of God. He also has a strong teaching anointing in the area of finance. Many have been blessed financially after following the principles taught in his finance and budgeting seminars.

Bishop Stanley Williams also has an Apostolic and Prophetic message for the Body of Christ and leaders.

He is a Pastor to Pastors and unselfishly imparts his anointing to those sent by God to learn from him. Bishop Williams brings individuals into the full awareness of their purpose and God's will for their life and their ministry.